Praise for *How to Make Things Faster*

Cary Millsap has a gift. Yes, he's brilliant at making things run faster, but his true genius is translating complex problems into simple, powerful ideas. This master teacher combines vivid stories with clear practices to teach principles that are as timeless as they are timely. If you want systems that keep pace with the new world of work, don't wait—read *How to Make Things Faster!*

—Liz Wiseman, New York Times *bestselling author of* Multipliers *and* Impact Players

You may think at first glance that *How to Make Things Faster* is a book about technology. It's not. While technology plays an important part, it's really a supporting player in the story of how people are impacted by technology. Looking at challenges from the perspective of end users is what makes *How to Make Things Faster* so insightful. Cary reminds us that in order to solve real performance challenges, we need to work on what's most important to the people who interact with the systems we design, build, and operate. You'll meet these people in *How to Make Things Faster*; and you'll come away with a new appreciation for *How to Make Things Faster* makes things better for all of us.

—*Dominic Delmolino, vice president at Amazon Web Services*

I can't believe I was in my forties the first time I saw how to optimize a system the way Cary and his team do it. Now, it doesn't even make sense to me that anyone would try it any other way.

—*Richard Russell, former 7-Eleven enterprise architect*

Every technology executive responsible for mission-critical systems should read *How to Make Things Faster*. It's one of the easiest and most entertaining reads you'll find, and it will prepare you thoroughly for handling—that is, solving *and* avoiding—technology performance crises.

—*Mark Sweeney, former technology executive at Bank of America*

How to Make Things Faster is a comfortable book. While Cary is a very skilled professional, he is also a gifted storyteller. He is one of the best presenters—technology or not—that you will come across, and this clearly comes through in *How to Make Things Faster*. It's both satisfying and refreshing to see him explain effortlessly, in normal English, these topics that so many people stumble over.

—*Guðmundur Jósepsson, director and performance specialist at Inaris*

I first met Cary almost 20 years ago when I took a class he taught on diagnosing Oracle database performance problems. That class changed my approach to diagnosing performance issues far beyond Oracle. It remains probably the best technical class I have taken in the past 40 years. Making things go fast is more than one's personal need for speed. Frequently, the speed with which a task can be completed will determine one's success or failure. *How to Make Things Faster* is filled with many deep insights which Cary has gained solving difficult, real-world performance problems throughout his career. He uses entertaining stories from many of his encounters to illustrate the points he is making. I highly recommend this book to all software professionals and anyone else whose work relies on making things go fast.

—*Andrew Zitelli, aerospace software engineer and IndyCar race enthusiast*

As Cary has written in *How to Make Things Faster*, "Getting people to do the right thing is almost always the hardest part of a project." That is not only true for IT projects but also for so many other activities. Hence, I highly recommend you to do the right thing by reading this book and let Cary share his wisdom with you. I am sure it will help you make things faster.

—Christian Antognini, author of
Troubleshooting Oracle Performance

I am not surprised that Cary wrote this book. I always expected it. He has so much to teach! *How to Make Things Faster* is easy to read, and the lessons are excellent. I love it.

—George Kadifa, managing director at Sumeru Equity Partners

Having known Cary for a number of years, worked with him for a few of those, and listened to a relatively large number of his presentations, a lot of the ideas in *How to Make Things Faster* were already familiar. What's new is the storytelling approach. One of the things I like best about the book is the way he boils down all the stories to the salient points: "Look at the right *it*," "Attack symptoms in priority order," etc. I think, in this book, it's done more clearly than I've ever seen anyone do it before.

—Doug Gault, senior software development manager at Oracle

When I first met Cary, he taught me not just about technology but about life. I still, to this day, use his words of wisdom in my interactions with family, coworkers, and friends. With *How to Make Things Faster*, Cary continues to educate and remind me, not just about how to improve technology but how to improve in life.

—Magnus Stjernström, software enthusiast

How to Make Things Faster

*Lessons in Performance from
Technology and Everyday Life*

Cary Millsap

Beijing · Boston · Farnham · Sebastopol · Tokyo

How to Make Things Faster

by Cary Millsap

Copyright © 2023 Cary Millsap. All rights reserved.

Published by O'Reilly Media, Inc., 1005 Gravenstein Highway North, Sebastopol, CA 95472.

O'Reilly books may be purchased for educational, business, or sales promotional use. Online editions are also available for most titles (*http://oreilly.com*). For more information, contact our corporate/institutional sales department: 800-998-9938 or *corporate@oreilly.com*.

Acquisitions Editor: Andy Kwan	**Indexer:** Ellen Troutman-Zaig
Development Editor: Melissa Potter	**Interior Designer:** Monica Kamsvaag
Production Editor: Katherine Tozer	**Cover Designer:** Susan Thompson
Copyeditor: Charles Roumeliotis	**Illustrator:** Kate Dullea
Proofreader: Piper Editorial Consulting, LLC	

June 2023:   First Edition

Revision History for the First Edition

2023-06-09:   First Release

See *http://oreilly.com/catalog/errata.csp?isbn=9781098147068* for release details.

The O'Reilly logo is a registered trademark of O'Reilly Media, Inc. *How to Make Things Faster*, the cover image, and related trade dress are trademarks of O'Reilly Media, Inc.

978-1-098-14706-8

[LSI]

To my Mom, who read every word.

Countless times.

Increasingly, people seem to misinterpret complexity as sophistication, which is baffling—the incomprehensible should cause suspicion rather than admiration.

—NIKLAUS WIRTH

Contents

Foreword

It's high time that Cary wrote this book. He has been teaching and practicing the material in *How to Make Things Faster* for a quarter of a century. I've read this book several times now. I think you're really going to enjoy it. It's the kind of book that can change your life. I know, because the principles that are explained within it have already changed mine. I got an 18-year head start, because the essence of *How to Make Things Faster* is the essence of *Optimizing Oracle Performance*, a book that Cary wrote with Jeff Holt in 2003. That essence is a method called "Method R."

Method R changed my life. It's the foundation of my professional career. Before I learned about it, I had studied and applied all the "usual" tips and tricks and tools and techniques that I was supposed to know in my role as a database administrator. I had some successes, but my results were inconsistent, and everything seemed complicated and difficult. Method R turned my idea of optimizing on its head almost instantly. Everything became clear and simple.

And not just Oracle things. With Method R, I could see clearly what information I needed to collect about anything I was supposed to improve. I could see where to find the root causes of performance issues, and how to fix them. The best thing, though, was that I was able to explain to others what I was doing and why. I found that especially fulfilling. I could do this because, with Method R, I wasn't guessing— I knew.

It turns out that lots of people actually saw the applicability of Method R beyond Oracle, but that 2003 book was definitely a book about Oracle. *How to Make Things Faster* is not. This is a book about *people* with decisions to make. Not just Oracle people, and not even just information technology people with long-running batch jobs and such, but anybody with a meal to cook or children to take to their sporting activities—anything you want to make faster, better, or more elegant. The same principles apply everywhere. When I first started applying Method R to my life, I remember thinking: "Can it really be this simple?" The answer is an unequivocal *yes*!

How to Make Things Faster is a comfortable book. While Cary is a very skilled professional, he is also a gifted storyteller. He is one of the best presenters—technology or not—that you will come across, and this clearly comes through in *How to Make Things Faster*. It's both satisfying and refreshing to see him explain effortlessly, in normal English, these topics that so many people stumble over. The stories relate to almost everyone's experience, whether their trade is IT or not. In this book, I think you will find at least a handful of stories that will make you go, "Yeah, I've been through this myself."

The stories are what lure you in, but it's the lessons that will change you. In *How to Make Things Faster*, you'll learn how the simple act of properly observing what is going on makes all the difference in the world. You'll learn how to identify, view, scope, analyze, and cure performance issues with confidence and consistency. You'll learn how to use the emotions of your colleagues as a force for Good. You'll learn how to test better, so that you can *avoid* problems instead of bumping your face on them later. You'll learn how to find hard evidence about whether further improvement is possible or not. You will know.

How to Make Things Faster is a textbook if you want it to be. It's also the kind of book that you can just read at random if you want. I think this book is going to help a lot of people just like you make a positive mark upon the world.

—*Guðmundur Jósepsson*
December 2021
Kópavogur, Iceland

Preface

Making things faster is about making things better. Making *life* better. The faster your tools can work, the more time you have for doing the things you *want* to be doing. If your tools help you process information, then the faster they work, the better decisions you can make.

Optimizing—whether a computer, or a plow, or anything in between—requires two separate skill sets: one, *asking* the right questions; and two, of course, *answering* those questions. Most people who think about optimizing are well aware of this second skill set. Fewer seem aware of the first one. But this first one—the mere act of asking the right questions—is the skill you need to develop first, especially if you're a leader. You might be surprised at how quickly you'll be able to learn it.

There's a problem, though. The questions I'll teach you to ask are simple. But anyone who's ever met an inquisitive child knows that simple questions aren't always easy to answer. For example, the people who look after your company's computer may know exactly what the system's CPU utilization looks like at 2:00 p.m. on a given Friday, but they may not be able to answer how long it takes a clerk to enter an order. There's a mismatch between the answers they'll want to give and the questions you'll want to ask. This mismatch itself hides opportunities to make things faster. I'll teach you how to find them.

Optimizing is often more political than technical. It's curious, then, that books about optimizing are almost always only technical. It's easy for technical people to regard the nontechnical elements of a project as unnecessary and maybe even ridiculous disruptions. But the fact is, the nontechnical aspects of optimizing require understanding and effort, just like the technical aspects do. To optimize something, sometimes you have to confront the monsters created by panic and fear, *in addition* to being productive technically. A strong track record of successes will help you win debates about what to do next, but you'll never be able to create that track record without exercising some political savvy.

My goal with this book is to help you improve both kinds of skills: the asking and the answering, the political and the technical. The payoff potential is huge. When you understand both the science of performance and the art of navigating the desires and emotions of the people who care about it, then you can optimize *anything*.

Acknowledgments

The bulk of what I accomplish as a human being is through the love and grace of my wife and children—Mindy, Alexander, Nikolas, and Cathryne—my parents Van and Shirle (I miss you, Dad), my wife's parents Ted and Evelyn, and my sister-in-law Alison.

This book wouldn't have been possible without Jeff Holt. It is difficult to imagine how much I'd have never learned without the time I've spent with Jeff since 1999.

I would like to thank everyone who's been part of my story, who has helped me, encouraged me, or inspired me over the past several years, including:

Steve Adams, Stephen Andert, Chris Antognini, Jon Bentley, Martin Berger, Richard Bonacci, Michael Brown, Mathew Butler, Steve Butterworth, Jerry Carlisle, Jae Choi, Mark Clark, Tom Corrado, Rudy Corsi, Ron Crisco, Chris Date, Lex de Haan, Dominic Delmolino, James Docherty, Ellen Dudar, Kevin Duffy, Nancy Dushkin, Larry Ellison, Jean Emerson, Dave Ensor, Michael Erwin, Eric Evans, Mark Farnham, Charlene Feldkamp, Ken Ferlita, Alyssa Freas, Doug Fricke, Doug Gault, Jonathan Gennick, Eli Goldratt, Gary Goodman, Alex Gorbachev, Donald Gross, Neil Gunther, Stephan Haisley, Tim Hall, Jimmy Harkey, Carl Harris, Frits Hoogland, Jonathan Intner, Lynn Isabella, Øyvind Isene, Raj Jain, Laurel Jamtgaard, Jarod Jenson, Guðmundur Jósepsson, Chet Justice, George Kadifa, Tom Kemp, Brian Kernighan, Larry Klein, Leonard Kleinrock, Donald Knuth, Stefan Koehler, Anjo Kolk, Toon Koppelaars, Brian Kush, Tom Kyte, Ray Lane, Jonathan Lewis, Debra Lilley, Bryn Llewellyn, Craig Martin, Connor McDonald, Brendan McNamee, Becki Memmer, Danny Menascé, Rick Minutella, James Morle, Karen Morton, Nils-Peter Nelson, Evelyn Neumayr, Craig Newburger, Mogens Nørgaard, Donald Norman, Kerry Osborne, Saul Padilla, Mauro Pagano, Harold Palacio, Tanel Põder, Darryl Presley, Marcin Przepiorowski, Ray Quiett, Willis Ranney, Mike Riley, Dennis Ritchie, Andy Rivenes, Allan Robertson, Jesse Ruder, Robert Rudzki, Richard Russell, Rachel Rutti, Martha Sabelhaus, Virag Saksena, Robyn Sands, Baron Schwartz, Gwen Shapira, Robert Shaw, Abdul Sheikh, Carlos Sierra, Kyle Smith, Nancy Spafford, Bryant Stavely,

Veronica Stigers, Jared Still, Magnus Stjernström, Mark Sweeney, James Thomson, Dan Tow, Edward Tufte, Hank Tullis, Delores Utley, Peter Utzig, Fidel Vales, Bill Walker, Mark Williams, Gerald Williamson, Liz Wiseman, Graham Wood, Scott Wyper, Steve Wyper, Winston Zhang, Andrew Zitelli, Jeff Zollars, neto from Brazil.

Conventions Used in This Book

The following typographical conventions are used in this book:

Italic
> Indicates new terms, URLs, email addresses, filenames, and file extensions.

`Constant width`
> Refers to program elements such as variable names and keywords.

O'Reilly Online Learning

 For more than 40 years, *O'Reilly Media* has provided technology and business training, knowledge, and insight to help companies succeed.

Our unique network of experts and innovators share their knowledge and expertise through books, articles, and our online learning platform. O'Reilly's online learning platform gives you on-demand access to live training courses, in-depth learning paths, interactive coding environments, and a vast collection of text and video from O'Reilly and 200+ other publishers. For more information, visit *https://oreilly.com*.

How to Contact Us

Please address comments and questions concerning this book to the publisher:

> O'Reilly Media, Inc.
>
> 1005 Gravenstein Highway North
>
> Sebastopol, CA 95472
>
> 800-889-8969 (in the United States or Canada)
>
> 707-829-7019 (international or local)
>
> 707-829-0104 (fax)
>
> *support@oreilly.com*
>
> *https://www.oreilly.com/about/contact.html*

We have a web page for this book, where we list errata, examples, and any additional information. You can access this page at *https://oreil.ly/make-things-faster*.

For news and information about our books and courses, visit *https://oreilly.com*.

Find us on LinkedIn: *https://linkedin.com/company/oreilly-media*.

Follow us on Twitter: *https://twitter.com/oreillymedia*.

Watch us on YouTube: *https://www.youtube.com/oreillymedia*.

PART I

Look at It

Bob

In the early 1990s, I worked for the consulting division of an up-and-coming database company called Oracle. My job was to fly to a different customer site each week and help the people there make their Oracle-based application systems run faster. I did this about 30 times a year.

My manager was named Robert. He was from Pittsburgh, and he had a small team of people like me spread throughout the US. At the time, he introduced himself as Bob, and he taught us how to say his nickname with just a tiny bit of *w* in there—"Bwob"—like his family and friends would say it. We felt like family on Bob's team. He was a great boss. He taught us a lot, and he always had our backs.

My job was a whole new world every week. Every Wednesday or so, I would call Bob (usually from a hotel), and he would tell me my mission for the following week: what airport to fly to, what hotel to stay at, whether I'd travel Sunday night or Monday morning, who'd be meeting with me and where, and what I'd be doing. Every week I wasn't at a client site, I was teaching or preparing to teach my colleagues what I was learning in the field.

In my earliest engagements on Bob's team, I would mostly execute tasks that Bob had defined for me before my trip. While I was at this week's client, Bob would be negotiating the tasks I'd be doing at next week's client. He'd tell me, "They're having disk I/O performance problems, so you'll be rebalancing their database files across a bunch of new disk drives that they've bought." Stuff like that. As you'll see, that formula would evolve over time.

All that flying around sounds like a nightmare to me now, but back then I was young and single, and I enjoyed the adventure. The technical challenges were interesting to me, and I accumulated a pretty solid record at solving them. That's no surprise, though, because I had the support of a whole company behind me. Bob was excellent at making sure I had access to everyone and everything I needed. I spent a lot of time with a lot of very helpful and smart people in Redwood Shores.

Still, the job was difficult, and not for the reasons you might initially think. The hardest problems were political, not technical. Often, the people I visited were openly hostile, not toward me personally, but toward the red logotype on my business card. But it had the same effect. Solving problems wasn't just about fixing software. There were these extra steps that were much more difficult. The job wasn't one step, it was four:

1. Listen. Let people explain their anger and frustration.
2. Calm them down so they can think clearly.
3. Convince them that you have a process they can trust.
4. Cure their anger and frustration.

The *calm* and *convince* steps were always the most demanding. In those early engagements, prescribing a process was tricky, because we didn't have one yet—my teammates and I were inventing process every week. Today, these four steps are the same, but now the *calm* and *convince* steps are a little bit easier because we have a decades-long track record of success. The track record helps especially in situations where the process runs counter to the client's instincts....And, as it turns out, a lot of people have really bad instincts about performance. I can help you with that one, if you'll keep reading.

Phyllis

In my earliest engagements, my manager Bob had prepared a list of specific tasks for me to work through when I got to the customer site. Over time, he would give me more latitude over deciding what those tasks should be. One engagement changed everything.

One Monday, as usual, my new client would show me the facility, introduce me to the people I'd be working with, and review the tasks that I'd be performing. After the meeting, a database administrator (DBA) escorted me to the desk where I would work for the next few days. I then set out to perform the task I had been assigned: to balance their database files across a bunch of new disk drives.

I was done mid-Wednesday, and I let everyone know that I was ready for them to test the system. Shortly after that, one of the managers introduced me to Phyllis (not her real name) and a handful of her colleagues. Phyllis was a leader in the accounting department. Her whole department, I now learned, had been unhappy with the system. Their unhappiness had in fact been the impetus for buying a bunch of new disk drives and soliciting my help. Phyllis's colleagues had come with her to watch the event that was about to unfold.

After the introductions, Phyllis sat down at a terminal to run the part of the application that she was the most upset about. Here's how it would go down: she would type some stuff, and if the thing that happened next wasn't fast enough, then my visit (at least my visit thus far) would be deemed a failure.

Gulp.

So we all stood there, nervously hoping that whatever this thing was would go fast. People crossed their fingers behind their backs. It was clear: this test was a big deal. I stood there, wondering what the hell she was running, and also why nobody had mentioned Phyllis to me on Monday. Or, better yet, last week. But now, here we were: if Punxsutawney Phyllis sees her shadow, then we all get six more weeks of winter. It was terrifying.

After some seconds passed, she turned around in her chair. There was a small grin, a little eyes-closed nod, and a thumbs-up. And then a great contentment did come over the land. The people she'd brought with her literally clapped. Softly, like at a golf tournament. People smiled at me and patted my shoulder and told me thank you.

I knew it wasn't meant to have been an ambush. There was a perfectly legitimate reason why nobody had introduced me to Phyllis or told me the real goal of my visit: I was just the file-balancer guy. I wasn't responsible for *deciding* what to do, I was just responsible for *doing* it. But if Phyllis's test hadn't turned out the way everyone had hoped, then of course there was no avoiding that I would be implicated in the failure. Just like I had been praised for her test succeeding, I would have been blamed if it had failed.

As it happened, I was lucky. If Phyllis's thing had originally been slow for any reason other than whatever changed when I rebalanced those files, then the thing she ran *wouldn't* have been faster.

Good luck is nice and all, but counting on luck is not how I wanted to run my career. So I explained to Bob: I needed to meet Phyllis and hear her story earlier. I needed to be part of the process for deciding what tasks get executed in my engagements.

Bob agreed. He was probably even proud of me for suggesting it. And thus did it come to pass: I would now be invited to the engagement planning calls, where I would learn about the *business motives* for each of my visits.

3

The Real Goal

What was the success criterion for the Phyllis story? I went into the engagement thinking that it was "Cary has successfully rebalanced our files on our new disks." But the client didn't really care about file balancing. Well, they did, but only insofar as it made Phyllis's thing run faster. They cared about file balancing *only* because they believed that file balancing would help Phyllis. File balancing wasn't their real *goal*, it was merely a potential *cure* that someone had proposed.

The lesson to learn here can be told in just three small words:

Look at it.

It sounds simple. I mean, how hard can it be to just look at something? But it's one of those things that's harder than it seems at first. Then, once you break a couple of bad habits, you realize that it really is easy after all.

To "look at it," you have to do two things:

- Figure out what the right *it* is.
- Figure out how to *look*.

The first step is usually a matter of just changing who you listen to. The second step requires tools. I'll be sharing lots of ideas with you about both.

4

Nancy

I met Nancy (her real name) in 1994 in Denver, Colorado. Again, on a Wednesday. Like a lot of companies I visited back then, the company she worked for had bought a big Oracle Financials software license.

The engagement started off in the typical way. I flew Monday morning into Stapleton Airport, drove to the office, and as soon as I got there, we had a big meeting. A dozen or more people ate donuts and drank coffee in a conference room until the meeting was called to order. DBAs and various technical specialists all sat together on the lefthand side of a long conference table. Users and system owners all sat together on the righthand side. I, their guest, sat at the head.

I took notes as people took turns telling stories about the system. The users went first. Richard (not his real name) was having a problem with some report he was running. I didn't recognize the name of the report; it was some kind of accounting thing. Julie (not her real name) was having a problem with some other application feature whose name I might have half-recognized. Nancy, who joined by speakerphone, explained her problems with some other thing. And on it went. I wrote down all the things that the users had told me they were having problems with.

When the DBAs and system administrators talked, it was the users' turn to only half-recognize the words in the conversation. I was much more comfortable in this part of the meeting, because now we were using words from *my* vocabulary—things like indexes and rollback segments and I/O. Of course, yes, I could certainly check all those things. I wrote them all down.

After an hour or so, it was meeting over, off to work. My host, a DBA, escorted me to the desk I'd be working at, showed me how to log in, and made sure I knew how to get in touch with everybody. I sat down and began my work.

Now, at this point in my career, the work I did for Oracle Financials sites was pretty much just the rote execution of a half dozen items on a list I had accumulated long before arriving. It almost didn't matter what anybody said in the Monday meeting. I would always listen politely and take notes, but I already knew most of what I was going to be doing. Almost every Financials site I'd ever visited had the same problems over and over again. The design of the product virtually assured that people would make certain configuration mistakes. I knew what those mistakes were, and I knew how to fix them.

And so I worked Monday and Tuesday, and by Wednesday mid-morning, I was ready for feedback. I had completed my checklist of things that I had hoped would address all of the users' concerns. I had looked at all the specific things that the technical people had asked me to look at. And I had written up my notes about what all I had done. Now it was time to hit the phone, to see how the users were doing.

First on my list was Richard, who had the slow report. "Hello, Richard, I don't know if you remember me. I'm Cary, the consultant from Oracle who is here to make your system faster. I am calling to find out if your [blah-blah] report is running any faster. You had mentioned Monday morning that it was taking more than twenty minutes to run, and this was a problem." Ah yes, the whatever-it-was report was running in less than five minutes now, and he was thrilled. I asked him if I could quote him on that in my report, and he consented. Excellent! One down, six to go.

My next call went exactly the same way: Julie was delighted, thank you; yes I could quote her in my report. I made a few other calls, and they all went the same way, just one dopamine hit after another. By the time I got to Nancy, I was pretty pleased with myself. A couple more of these calls, and I might be able to head home a day or two early.

But on the call with Nancy, I wasn't getting the nice, love-you vibe that I had been getting on the other calls. I tried to get the affirmation: "But doesn't the pop-up account code validation run a lot faster now, since I've been here?"

She said it does.

"Okay, then, can I quote you on that?"

"…Well, you can, but I don't really *care* very much about that. What *I* care about is the [blah-blah] field of the [blah-blah] form."

Oh man… She wasn't happy yet, and I didn't even understand the words she was using to describe why. But I did know what to do. Bob had taught me that a long time ago. So I asked her, "Well, do you mind if I come visit you, so that I can *see* exactly what you're talking about?"

She said, well, I *could*...if I really wanted to, but..."Oh, of course, I'm happy to do it!" I told her.

"Well," she said, "I'm not in the building you're in. I'm a couple miles away."

Not a problem, I told her. I had a rental car and could head over right away. So she gave me directions to her building and said she'd meet me at the security desk. I asked her to please tee up her problem in the application while I was driving so she could show me exactly what's bothering her when I got there. She said she'd be ready.

So I packed up my briefcase and went outside to my car. I was a little nervous about what would happen when I got there. What if I put her through all this trouble and couldn't figure out how to help? But I knew it would be fine in the end. By that time, I had learned that there's no real shame in saying, "I don't know, but I can help you find out." She had a phone on her desk. I knew lots of people I could call if I needed a hand.

The drive didn't take long. Nancy met me at security just like she'd promised. She signed me in, and we walked up the stairs to the second floor. On the way to her cube, she showed me the biggest Xerox machine that I had ever seen. She explained that this huge ten-yard-long printer/photocopier could take a floppy disk in its east end and then birth a bound book out its west end. We nodded hello to the mail guy who was pushing a cart down her hallway.

Seeing Nancy's cube told a story that I never would have seen through the phone. On her wall hung a certificate of achievement declaring that Nancy could type over 100 words per minute. Attached to the right side of her DEC VT320 terminal was a plastic clipboard. She had two spikes with weighted bases (called *spindles*, I later learned—as in "do not fold, spindle, or mutilate"). One, on her desk to the right of her terminal, was labeled "IN." Another one, on her desk to the left of her terminal, was labeled "OUT."

I could envision her workflow. Papers would load up on her IN spike. (Carefully, I hope: those spindles look like a bloodbath waiting to happen.) She'd pull a page off the IN spike onto the clipboard and then type 100 words per minute for a little while. Then she'd move the page from the clipboard to the OUT spike. She'd probably repeat this until the IN spike was empty. Then she'd probably file everything on the OUT spike.

Everything looked optimized for speed. This was my first impression.

Then Nancy explained, "I pay bills. You saw the mail guy. He brings bills to me from the daily mail. The one bill that I dread the most is from Xerox. I just got one today. The huge copy machine I showed you just outside there? We pay Xerox every month for it. The reason I hate the Xerox bill is because I can never remember the vendor name that I have to call up in the application. I can never remember from one month to the next whether it's just 'Xerox' or 'Xerox Inc.' or 'Xerox Corporation'…here's what I have to do to pay the Xerox bill."

Then she turned around in her seat and put her hands on the keyboard. The Xerox bill was clipped into her clipboard. Her cursor was positioned in the *vendor name* field. She had teed up her problem, just like I had asked on the phone. Then she typed the characters \ Q R. The backslash dropped down an application menu, simulated with box-drawing characters, like ┌, ─, and ┐ . The Q dropped down a *query* menu, and the R *ran* a "blind" (meaning unrestricted) query. Thus, \ Q R instructed the application to return every vendor name on the whole entire system. On the screen was the first page of the result of this query, containing about twenty vendor names all beginning with the letter *A*.

Then Nancy turned her face toward me and, with her righthand index finger, she started tapping the Next Screen key. She moved her lips quickly, "One-two-three-four-five-six-seven-eight…" as she was doing it, and when she got to twenty-six she stopped. "Twenty-six times I have to hit the Next Screen key to get to where Xerox is listed." Of course, she knew it was twenty-six only because she had just rehearsed it while I was driving over.

The application couldn't keep up with Nancy's Next Screen key presses. The screen would refresh in lunges. It would fill half the screen, pause for a second, and then fill-*pause*-fill-fill-*pause*. It would fill and pause like that for tens of seconds. It felt like forever.

Finally, after paging through the whole vendor name table, her screen showed the final few vendor names:

```
Walton Group
Wortmann AG
Xerox Corp
Xircom Inc
Xylog
Zimmermann's Deli
```

She clicked the ↓ key a couple times, highlighting the row that said Xerox, and she said, "There you go."

So, apparently it's "Xerox Corp," no period at the end.

She stood up politely, in case I wanted to take her seat, and crossed her arms. My heart was racing, because I *knew* this one, and it was going to be really easy to fix. I wasn't going to need to sit down. I did need to choose my words carefully, though, because I didn't want to sound disrespectful by blurting out something about how "easy" this was going to be, after it had been plaguing her for so long.

I smiled, and after what I hope seemed like only a second or two, I found the right words. "Nancy," I said, "in about two minutes, I think you're going to be *really* happy." She smiled at that and invited me to tell her what I had in mind. I motioned for her to sit back down.

"Please go back to where you were when I first got here, back to the field where you type the vendor name." A couple of backslash-this and backslash-thats, and she was back to the *vendor name* field. I asked her, "Now, please type x (the first letter of 'Xerox')." She did. "And now press Return." And then *boom*. Instantly:

```
Xerox Corp
Xircom Inc
Xylog
```

She snapped around, hands to her cheeks. "Oh my gosh, are you kidding me?! Are you *kidding* me!" Big grins all around.

I told her that the application had this feature where if you type just the first few letters of a value you want to find and press Return, then the software automatically displays the results of a pattern match, using what you've typed as a prefix. She kept grinning and shaking her head. "I'm going to schedule a department meeting right away, because everybody on the whole floor is having the same kind of problem I was having."

…Everybody on the whole floor.

We enjoyed the celebration for a couple more minutes. I asked if there was anything else, and she told me no that was it. She said she appreciated the other stuff I had fixed, too (she *had* noticed it), but this was the big one. It was why she had hated this new system.

…Hated this new system.

5

Looking at the Right It

How could a problem like Nancy's have persisted for everyone in a whole *department*, for however long they'd been suffering with it? Was it just the distance between buildings? Being physically separated didn't help, but that's not really the biggest contributor to the problem. I've been too many places where the same kinds of problems were happening just down the hall. Technical people just tend not to visit their users. In Nancy's specific case, you could say that if she and I hadn't *both* been a little stubborn, then there wouldn't have been a fun story called "Nancy" in this book.

I understand, I really do. It takes guts to walk down the hall and ask whether everything's OK, when you know that, one, you might get an earful, and two, you might not be able to do anything about it. Because, after all, what do you know about accounting—or manufacturing, or retail, or aircraft landing gear maintenance, or garbage truck scheduling? But with practice, talking to users becomes a habit, and it doesn't bother you anymore. And you become a more valuable player to the business.

Remember: there's always, "I don't know, but I can help you find out." It's the leadership thing to do.

So on the very first morning of my engagement in Denver, Nancy was right there on the speakerphone, explaining her problem to us. But I just didn't get it. Her explanation didn't fit into any of the predefined slots in my brain about Oracle Financials performance. But I knew that whatever her problem was, I needed to understand it, so I could either help or get help. My visit couldn't be successful without helping Nancy.

Of course, I didn't know I was looking at the other end of Nancy's problem on Tuesday, when I stood in the server room with a bunch of guys all scratching our heads about how to pump vendor names down a wire to another building as fast as we could. In that server room, nobody knew that the people in the other building didn't want all those names in the first place. We talked about making Oracle's multiblock read count bigger. We actually discussed the possibility that they might need to *buy more network bandwidth.*

But the real performance problem wasn't in the server room or the network cable; it was two miles away, in Nancy's cubicle. We were looking at the right problem in the server room: we were just looking at the wrong end of it. We needed to be looking at the problem from the *symptom* perspective, the way the users see it. I never would have solved Nancy's problem if I hadn't seen what she was typing.

Go where the symptom is.

The lesson in Denver was not just to *look at it*, but to make sure that we're paying attention to the *it* that's at the *symptom* end of the problem.

6

When You Can't Look at It

It makes sense: go where the symptom is, see what the user sees. But what if you can't? What if Nancy isn't two miles away but two hundred? What if your users are speckled across 30+ time zones? Then what? There are many answers. Here are a few:

Screen sharing

If we'd had Zoom in 1994 (and also, you know, *laptops*), I could have solved Nancy's problem without a visit. Zoom would have been enough. The COVID-19 pandemic has proven that, often, Zoom is enough.

Telemetry

If you really want to know what people all over the world are feeling when they're using your software, then measure and record the experiences those people are having. Measure and record things like:

- What is the name of the feature being measured?
- When did the execution of the feature begin?
- When did the execution end?
- Who executed it?
- Where did the execution take place?
- How much work did the execution do?
- What is the return status of the execution?

Then, when someone has a miserable experience, it'll show up in your data, where you can *look at it* from the *symptom* perspective. And when you fix it, *that* will show up in your data. Application features that record such information make an application more *observable*.

Simulations

Set up application access that will allow you to simulate the experiences your users are having with your system. You can, for example, artificially impair your network connection to better simulate how that user who is 3,000 miles away experiences your system.

Seeing your system as your users experience it is the starting point to a method that keeps your priorities aligned with your business's priorities.

PART II

Method

7

Forty-Nine Grievances

One sunny Texas Saturday morning in 1998, I was mowing my lawn on my little green and yellow John Deere tractor. When I turned for a pass toward the back door, I could see that my wife was walking toward me, making that slash-across-the-throat motion that meant shut it down. I had a phone call. Normally, she wouldn't have interrupted my yard work, but this was Ray Lane. Ray was the president and chief operating officer of Oracle Corporation. He was my boss's boss. He had never called me before.

A customer in Southern California was having some crippling performance problems. They couldn't take orders, they couldn't ship orders, they couldn't process return merchandise authorizations…they couldn't really do much of anything. This was a multibillion-dollar company, and these problems were costing them millions of dollars every day. Ray told me that at the trajectory they were on, they would be out of business by Friday.

And here's why it was Ray calling instead of someone else: this company had made it clear to the COO of Oracle Corporation that if *they* went out of business, they would "do everything in their power to take Oracle down with them." Ray told me to assemble my team Sunday evening in Orange County, with anybody at Oracle I wanted to take with me. I did.

We assembled Sunday night at our hotel. On Monday morning, my dream team and I walked through the doors of a profoundly broken company. Everything was hard, even the easy things. Even getting into the building through security was hard. Finding a place where my team could work was especially difficult, because all the conference rooms were already filled with teams of attorneys, all preparing for the big mutual annihilation deathmatch planned for Friday.

But the company had done one important thing right: they had listed all their problems. They didn't call them *problems* or *issues* like everybody else; they called them *grievances*. The word *grievance* was in play because it is a legal term of art that implies wrongdoing. And that's how they perceived Oracle: as having *wronged* them.

So, on a whiteboard in a public space where everyone on the project could see it, they had listed the most grievous twenty or so of their forty-nine total grievances (all of which had also been recorded in a spreadsheet). Each grievance had a name, a priority, a status, a brief description, and a list of the people who were working on it. I wish we had a prioritized list of grievances everywhere we go. It was a great idea that helped us really hit the ground running.

After studying the list with my team, we split into small groups to go attack the highest-priority items in parallel. The item that I assigned to myself was "Can't print shipping labels."

8

The Shipping Labels Problem

None of the issues in Orange County seemed easy at first. Everything was confused and disorganized everywhere we looked. But a little bit of asking around identified a customer employee who knew about the printing problem. He and I paired up to go figure it out. The first thing I asked him was the "let's look at the system" question of how long this process had been running. He showed me a form on the Oracle Manufacturing applications dashboard that showed job statuses, and it looked like the label printer job had completed a long time ago.

Well, that wasn't much help, so now what?

"So, how do we know that the labels aren't printing?" I asked.

"Because the guys down at the dock don't have labels."

"Can you take me to the dock?"

So off to the dock we went, to visit the symptom.

The dock was in the same building, just a two-minute walk away. It was physically configured like every other dock I had seen: warehouse over here, loading bays over there, with a staging area in between. Forklifts would bring pallets of boxes from the warehouse to the staging area for labeling, and then the drivers would load the boxes onto their trucks. The weird thing about *this* dock, though, was that nothing was moving. At least half a dozen drivers from UPS, FedEx, US Mail, DHL, and the warehouse employees were just sitting on the stacks of boxes, drinking coffee and talking about yesterday's games.

"Why are these guys sitting around?" I asked.

"They can't load the trucks until the boxes have labels on them."

"Where's the printer?" I asked.

It was right there in the middle of the staging area, a little printer about the size of a loaf of bread, screwed to a welded steel stand that was bolted to the floor. The stand raised it up waist-high, where people could pull the printed labels off the back of the printer without having to stoop down. It sat there, dead quiet, with a big fresh roll of blank labels loaded into it. The cable from the printer was zip-tied to the steel stand down to the floor, and it stretched across the floor, taped down with gaffer's tape, leading to an office door and then passing beneath it.

"Can we go in there?" I asked.

Yes we can.

Behind the door was a little table with an IBM PC-style microcomputer sitting on it. The cable from the printer was plugged into the back. My host explained that this computer was connected to the MicroVAX computer on the other side of the room, via FTP. The MicroVAX was connected to the main computer where the job to print the labels had already finished running. The screensaver had taken over the PC, whose screen was solid black. I asked my guide if he could press the Shift key so we could see what this thing was doing. He did. It looked like this:

```
C:\>
```

"Oh no," he shook his head. "We rebooted the machine last night, and apparently nobody thought to restart the FTP server."

"Can we start the FTP server right now?" I asked.

He was already typing. After a couple of seconds, I could hear *zit-zit-zzzzzzit-zit-zit* from the staging area. And thus did labels begin to stream forth from the printer. It was as if you had snapped your fingers, and the whole warehouse had broken out of its hypnosis. The warehouse staff started putting labels on boxes, and the drivers started loading boxes onto trucks.

Now they can ship.

"There needs to be an automated procedure for restarting the FTP server after a reboot," I said.

Nods.

The moral of this story? *Go where the symptom is,* and *look at it.…*At the actual symptom. Not a side effect, not a surrogate that's easier to measure, but the actual thing itself. In our case, the actual thing was not a form on a screen that says the label print job is complete. It was the printer on the dock.

9

More Grievances

Of course, fixing the label printing problem remedied only one of the forty-nine grievances (*remedied* is another legal term). There were forty-eight others. While I was in the warehouse looking at the label printer, my teammates were looking at other users' grievances. Team 2 was researching why the application was taking an average of twenty minutes to return an order confirmation number. The impact of that one was astounding, too:

Our customer's sales rep
> "Thank you for calling, how may I help you?"

Our customer's customer
> "Hi, yes. I'd like to place this week's $6,000,000 order. Here are the details…"

Sales rep
> "Thank you for your order. Unfortunately, our new system is really slow right now. I'm going to need to put you on hold for a few minutes before I can issue your order confirmation ID."

Buyers were getting sick of wasting half an hour every time they placed an order. Some of them were threatening to find a new supplier.

The Team 2 attack plan was, of course, the same as mine had been: to *look at* the problem *from the user's perspective*. They did this by tracing the sales order program. *Tracing* shows in detail how a program spends its time.

The trace showed that the program was awaiting the release of a lock that had been created by a custom sales report. The lock prevented anyone from inserting, updating, or deleting rows in the sales order table while the report was running. Since the report ran almost continuously during business hours (several times per day, forty minutes per execution), there was pretty much never a time during the day when order processing went smoothly.

Team 2 discovered that the report didn't even need the lock to run properly, so they removed its *lock table* command. This simple cure concluded another important scene in the overall horror show. Now our customer could take orders without foisting weird, frustrating delays upon their buyers.

Forty-nine is a lot of problems. Many of them were caused by badly written custom SQL. This was a second big problem for the forty-minute custom sales report. It was taking far longer and consuming far more resources than it should have. Another team fixed that problem later in the project.

We also found user errors, like salespeople unwittingly creating sales reports for the entire post-Napoleonic era (using a start date of negative infinity) instead of just for the present month. A little training solved this issue, though a better interface design probably could have prevented it from ever occurring.

Yet other problems were caused by poor operational discipline. For example, some programs were scored as grievances because they weren't finishing on time, but the real problem was that they weren't *starting* on time. The users couldn't run them because the company's automatic password expiration software had left them unable to log in to their system.

These are all problems that you really can't solve unless you *look* at them. Not through the lens of some system management tool, but through the lens of the actual individual human beings who are suffering to get their work done.

That first Monday was a big day for our whole team—both the customer and my consultants. By the time our Monday evening status meeting started, we had made enough progress that the business owners could enjoy the feeling of legitimate hope again. In just a day, we had removed some of their highest-priority business obstacles.

10

Priority

Understanding how to deal with lots of problems that come at you all at once is why our project in Orange County accomplished so much so quickly. When we arrived on site, nearly everything was a mess, but our client had nailed one really smart step. They had prepared a *prioritized* list of the *symptoms* they were experiencing. It looked like this:

Symptom	Priority
S1. Can't print shipping labels	1
S2. Can't confirm orders	1
S3. ...	2
...	...
S49. ...	5

The symptom column told us what we needed to do. The priority column told us what we needed to do *next*. That list is what got us off to such a fast start.

Priorities don't have to be unique. In Orange County, both order shipping and order booking were top-priority symptoms. They were both ranked at priority one, because they were equal barriers to surviving past Friday.

It is OK for two or more symptoms to have the same priority, but it leaves open the question of which symptom you should work on first. If you have more than one team (I had half a dozen little teams in Orange County), then you can work on more than one top-priority symptom at the same time. You can in fact work simultaneously on as many top-priority symptoms as you have parallel, independent teams.

But if you have more top-priority symptoms than you have teams to work on them, then you have to choose which symptom is 1.a and which one is 1.b. If you need information to break a tie, then do a surface-level diagnosis of all of the same-priority symptoms before deep-diving into any of them. Learn which one you believe you can relieve the soonest.

In Orange County, we were lucky to have their prioritized list of grievances. It saved us a lot of time. Some companies won't have that list until you coach them through discovering the information for themselves, and of course, that takes valuable time.

The key to such a process is to remember the goal: to determine which symptoms are the most important ones to fix *first*. Being low on the list doesn't mean a symptom won't get relieved; it just means that it probably won't get relieved *next*. Remember, the longer you spend discussing priorities, the longer it's going to be before you can begin providing relief.

11

But My Whole System Is Slow

Sometimes, when you ask people for a list of symptoms, they'll answer, "Everything. Literally everything is slow." No matter whether it's one specific symptom, or forty-nine, or literally everything, you need a list of symptoms that you can reproduce and diagnose.

Once, a client with an everything-is-slow problem got a little frustrated with my insistence that we identify just one program to start with. I persisted until he finally said, with some exasperation, that even executing a trivial SQL statement to return the system date was slow. "Excellent," I said, "then let's trace *that*!" I know he was thinking the idea was ridiculous, but it was easy to do. He humored me, and he traced it.

The trace immediately revealed a bug. The patch for this bug was already listed in the pile of dozens of recommendations that various people had offered. However, none of those recommendations were scheduled for implementation any time soon, because there'd been no apparent cause-effect linkage between any of the recommendations and the troubles they'd been having. Our trace, of course, was sufficient evidence to escalate the urgency of the patch idea.

I don't think anyone ever actually told me how many symptoms were relieved by applying the patch. It was almost certainly more than just the one SQL statement that he had traced.

12

Collateral Benefit

Here are the steps I've covered so far for starting a performance improvement project:

1. List the symptoms for which the business needs relief (report's too slow, can't find "Xerox" fast enough, can't print shipping labels…).
2. Sort the list into business priority order.

The next step is to dig in and get going:

3. For each symptom in the sorted list, look at it, find out why it consumes the time that it does, and cure its cause to relieve the symptom.

The job is to determine the cause of each symptom. There may be some hypotheses about each cause (as Phyllis's company had hypothesized that disk I/O was the cause of her slow report), but it is vital to determine positively that *this* is the cause of *that* before you start "fixing" things. So, where do you begin?

You begin right here, with your prioritized list of symptoms:

Symptom	Priority	Status (team)	Cause
S1	1	Open	?
S2	1	Open	?
…	…	…	…

So, imagine that you have two teams T1 and T2. Imagine that team T1 relieves symptom S1 by curing cause C1, and, working in parallel, team T2 relieves symptom S2 by curing cause C2. Then you can update your list:

Symptom	Priority	Status (team)	Cause
S1	1	~~Open~~ Resolved (T1)	~~?~~ C1
S2	1	~~Open~~ Resolved (T2)	~~?~~ C2
...	... ...		...

Now imagine that there's some other symptom S14 sitting way down the list at priority 4, and that—out of the blue—the users who've been experiencing symptom S14 unexpectedly report that S14 is resolved now, too.

So you can mark S14 as resolved. Since teams T1 and T2 both did work that could have affected S14, you won't know (without studying it a little bit) which team or which cause made the difference. But you do at least know it was something that team T1 or T2 did when they were working on causes C1 and C2, so you should record that:

Symptom	Priority	Status (team)	Cause
S1	1	Resolved (T1)	C1
S2	1	Resolved (T2)	C2
...	... ...		...
S14	4	~~Open~~ Resolved (T1 or T2)	~~?~~ C1 or C2
...	... ...		...

It is called a *collateral benefit* when curing the cause for one symptom serendipitously relieves some other symptom. It happens when two separate symptoms are the result of a single, shared cause.

Collateral benefit is common. For example, when you patch a bug that fixes a trivial query to return the system date, you help other queries, too. When you replace a program's algorithm with a more efficient one, you help not just the program you're working on, but also all the other programs on your system that compete for resources against the program you improved.

In Orange County, the lock on the sales order table blocked not just the high-priority program for creating new orders, but also the lower-priority program for updating existing orders:

Symptom	Cause
S1. Can't print shipping labels	C1. FTP server not restarted
S2. Can't confirm orders	C2. Sales order table locked
...	...
S14. Can't update orders	C2. Sales order table locked

When there's collateral benefit, the business gets to decide how much analysis you should devote to answering the question of where the collateral benefit came from. In Orange County, it was easy to figure out that it was the lock (C2) that had also been causing the inability to update orders (S14). But sometimes, it's not so easy.

So, should you bother with analyzing your symptom S14, which now is not even repeatable? The answer is at least *maybe*. Your curiosity is an important reason you're good at your job. And knowledge is power: maybe knowing the cause of symptom S14 will help you prevent recurrences of it. But if there are other high-priority symptoms to be relieved, then you should probably go help solve those problems first. You can come back to the curious case of S14 when things calm down.

13

The Silver Bullet

One of the obstacles you may run into is the *silver bullet* expectation. The silver bullet expectation is the belief that no matter how many problems you're feeling—say, for example, forty-nine—then there must be some switch you can flip, maybe a knob you can turn, that will solve them all. It's the assumption that all your symptoms share a common cause, that *everything* will be collateral benefit.

But that assumption can cause problems. What if, in fact, there *isn't* a single cause for all the different symptoms people are feeling? Looking for something that's not there wastes time and erodes morale.

In Orange County, for example, we never would have gotten anywhere if we'd fixated on the riddle, "What single cause could possibly be messing up label printing, order taking, and forty-seven other things all at the same time?" There's no sense getting mired in it. It's an unanswerable question, because there *wasn't* a single cause for all those symptoms. It's just how things were.

There's just no need to ever ask such a question. Whether or not there's a silver bullet waiting in your future shouldn't change your approach one way or the other. You need to start with the prioritized "list of grievances" either way. If curing the first symptom collaterally fixes everything else, then you can rejoice in your good luck. If your first cure doesn't fix everything all at once, then you'll move on to the new highest-priority symptom and continue from there.

14

The List

One of the most important attributes you can bring to a team is a sense of *relevance*. Relevance is the awareness of what matters and what doesn't. An irrelevant action is like a hammer swing that misses the nail. The secret to keeping your performance work relevant is simple:

Always diagnose the business's top-priority symptom first.

That prioritized list of symptoms is essential. Without it, it's hard to be valuable.

For example, imagine that you've been invited to do a system *health check*. There's no prioritized list of symptoms to work from. You're just supposed to look at the system holistically and identify everything that looks suspicious about how it's configured and how it's running.

Let's say you find something really interesting, like a missing index, an absurd parameter setting, a poorly connected controller board...something that smells indisputably important. And let's say you fix it. OK, great. So now: how will you know whether your fix matters or not? Do you remember the answer?

They're going to introduce you to Phyllis. She's going to run some report you've never heard of, and it's going to dawn on you that, ah, that list we never made: we're making it now, and Phyllis's report is apparently on it, along with who knows what else. And of course you're nervous whether your fix will matter at all to her report, because you have no idea how that report spends its time.

So, what happens if your health check identifies dozens of potential cure opportunities? Which one should you try first? It's hard to know:

- You can't use priority as a tool, because cures themselves don't *have* priorities, except for the ones they inherit from the symptoms they relieve. But if you don't have a prioritized list of symptoms, then you're stuck.

- You could try the least expensive cures first. But being less expensive doesn't make a cure more likely to work; it just softens the blow if it fails.

- Of course, you *want* to choose the cure that's most likely to be effective. But it's nearly impossible, even for experts, to predict the effect of some proposed cure upon a big system with "a lot of problems" that you don't have a list of.

This inability to predict the effect of a proposed cure is how companies end up with piles of recommendations they can't use, like my friend who needed the patch. But when you work from a prioritized list of symptoms, it's easy to prove the cause-effect relationship between your idea and something that matters to the business. You can even quantify it.

The high-priority "Can't confirm orders" symptom in Orange County is a good example. A trace showed that a lock was wasting up to 40 minutes of each book-an-order experience. That lock was why the sales reps were so frustrated, and why they were at risk of losing their biggest customers. The trace proved it beyond a shadow of a doubt.

You don't get proofs like that the other way around. Someone doing a health check while those sales reps were suffering might well have measured their busy system with thousands of users as spending less than 1% of its total time waiting on locks. Certainly, using *that* as evidence, you can't pitch the idea that locks are relevant to the business. If we hadn't driven our analysis from the list of prioritized symptoms, we'd have missed this one.

15

Method R

The performance improvement approach that I've been building through these stories I've been telling is actually a formal method with a name. It's called Method R. The R stands for *response time*. It's a response-time–oriented method because "My program takes too long to run" is a common way that you'll see symptoms expressed. But Method R is also useful for optimizing *throughput*, which is a measure of how many executions you can complete in a given time interval.

You've seen enough by now that the complete method will be no surprise:

1. List the symptoms for which the business needs relief.

2. Sort the list into business-priority order.

3. For each symptom S in the sorted list:

4.   While further relief for S is your top priority:

5.   Observe S (*look at it!*), ideally, in the act of misbehaving.

6.   Find the cause C of the misbehavior.

7.   Relieve S by curing C.

By now, I've pleaded my case for the importance of working on symptoms in business-priority order, and I've told a few stories about how to observe a symptom by *looking at it*. Not every problem is going to be as immediately evident as Nancy's problem or the label-printer adventure in Orange County. Over the next several chapters, I'll go into more detail about what you should be observing when your symptom is a slow computer program.

PART III

Profiling

16

Payroll

In October 1999, I left Oracle Corporation to start a new company with a former MBA classmate. In early 2001, one of our company's sales reps had made contact with a company headquartered in Dallas. He explained the point of our company and asked if there was anything we could do to help them. They told him not right now, but they'd keep our number in case something came up.

In September, something came up.

For several months, this company had been unable to pay their employees on time every payday because their Oracle Payroll system was too slow. The employees were getting so infuriated that some of them were coming in over the weekend and tearing the place up, vandalizing company property in protest over not getting paid on time.

The company had been fighting this problem for a long time, so the management team had decided to just bite the bullet and spend whatever it took to fix the situation and get back to normal. So, on the weekend of September 8–9, they upgraded all the 700 MHz CPUs in their database server to 1 GHz CPUs. The new CPUs were 1.46 times faster than the old ones, so the intention had been that Payroll should run 1.46 times faster.

But it didn't. And it was even worse than you think. After having spent all that time and money on an expensive CPU upgrade, Payroll on Monday was running *even slower* than it had before the upgrade. It wasn't just "not as much faster as we'd hoped"; it was "*actually worse than before.*" They were absolutely baffled. Nothing made sense anymore; could we please come visit? So we scheduled a visit. My colleague Jeff Holt and I would meet their technical team.

Here's what they knew:

- The problem with Payroll was a program called PYUGEN that was running too slowly. PYUGEN was a standard Oracle Payroll program that ran right on the database server whose CPUs had been upgraded.

- For months, their system monitoring tools had shown that when PYUGEN ran, the system was running at nearly 100% of its CPU capacity. This is what had given them the idea to upgrade their CPUs.

- The same monitoring tools had shown that when PYUGEN ran, the second-most dominant time consumer for the Oracle Database was an internal event called "latch free." They knew what "latch free" was, but they couldn't quite work out why PYUGEN needed so much of it.

Our sorted list of symptoms was clear. It had just one item: PYUGEN. So it was time to observe PYUGEN—our *look at it* step—in the act of misbehaving. We asked when they'd next be running it. The IT director laughed and said, "Around here, we're *always* running PYUGEN."

"Right now?" we asked. "Yes, right now," he said.

We explained that we weren't interested yet in looking at their system monitoring tools, that what we really wanted to do was *trace* PYUGEN's database process while it ran. Tracing is a standard Oracle Database feature that causes a database process to write a detailed log of all the subroutine calls it makes as it executes. It's exactly the kind of detail that we need to find out why a program like PYUGEN consumes the time it does.

We traced PYUGEN for about half an hour. It ran for longer than that, but a half hour's worth of trace data would be enough to show us what we wanted to see. We used one of our new company's products to aggregate the trace file into the following table:

Subroutine	Duration seconds	%	Count	Mean
SQL*Net message from client	984.010	50.3%	95,161	0.010 340
SQL*Net more data from client	418.820	21.4%	3,345	0.125 208
db file sequential read	279.340	14.3%	45,084	0.006 196
CPU service, EXEC calls	136.880	7.0%	67,888	0.002 016
CPU service, PARSE calls	74.490	3.8%	10,098	0.007 377
CPU service, FETCH calls	37.320	1.9%	57,217	0.000 652
latch free	23.690	1.2%	34,695	0.000 683
8 other subroutines	2.920	0.1%	111,829	0.000 026
Total (15)	1,957.470	100.0%	425,317	0.004 602

These subroutine names are Oracle-specific, but you're not going to need to understand any of them to follow along with the story. You should be able to answer all of the following questions without knowing *anything* about Oracle:

1. How long did PYUGEN run?

The duration for which we traced it was 1,957.470 seconds. That's a little more than 32 minutes.

2. What if you could eliminate all the "CPU service" calls? How much time would you save?

You'd save 248.69 seconds (136.880 + 74.490 + 37.320), which is 12.7% of the traced duration.

3. What if you could eliminate all the "latch free" calls?

You'd save 23.690 seconds, which is 1.2% of the traced duration.

4. How did PYUGEN spend most of its time?

PYUGEN spent most of its time calling the two "SQL*Net" subroutines listed in the first two lines of the profile. The first one consumed 50.3% of the traced duration. The top two together consumed 71.7%.

5. If you wanted to make PYUGEN run twice as fast, where would you begin?

You would figure out what these "SQL*Net" things are, and how to either (a) make PYUGEN call them fewer times, or (b) make each call to those subroutines take less time. There's no other way to do it.

We like to choose option *a* when we can, for reasons I'll explain in future chapters, but in this case, option *a* was not available to us. This application didn't provide a parameter for adjusting the network round-trip count, and we weren't going to be able to change the application's source code to make fewer round trips.

At this point in the project, we had to know a little bit about how Oracle works. After seeing the data, Jeff almost immediately suggested that the 0.010 340-second mean duration for the "SQL*Net message from client" subroutine calls looked suspicious. He told us that two programs that run on the same server shouldn't require 10-millisecond round trips.

He was able to prove this point within about 15 minutes' worth of testing with the DBA. He showed that each "SQL*Net message from client" call could be made 55 times faster by changing a parameter in a network configuration file.[1] They projected that making each call 55 times faster would make the total "SQL*Net message from client" duration drop from 984 seconds to less than 20 seconds, which would reduce PYUGEN's total duration by about half. This was a good enough idea to implement, without even considering the possible collateral benefit to the "SQL*Net more data from client" item in the second row of the table.

The whole visit lasted only about four hours. I was a little disappointed when we left, because they couldn't implement our suggestion right away. Of course, they needed the relief, but not at the expense of forsaking their change control process. A few days later, the DBA called to let us know that they had tested and implemented the cure we had suggested. As we had predicted, PYUGEN was now processing more than twice as many paychecks per minute as before, and they were very happy with that.

Now they could pay people on time.

…And, I guess, begin to repair their labor relations problem.

---

1 Cary Millsap and Jeff Holt, *Optimizing Oracle Performance: A Practitioner's Guide to Optimizing Response Time* (Sebastopol, CA: O'Reilly, 2003), 326–333; Cary Millsap (with Jeff Holt), *The Method R Guide to Mastering Oracle Trace Data* (Southlake, TX: Method R, 2019), 177–183.

17

The Sequence Diagram

A *sequence diagram* is a type of graph used to show the interactions between objects in the sequential order that those interactions occur. It's a picture that makes it easier to visualize response time. Here is a sequence diagram for the Payroll problem:

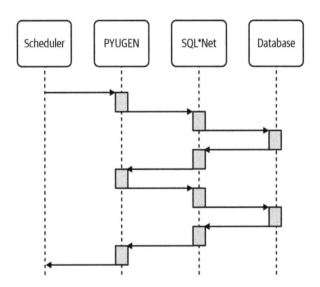

The vertical lines in a sequence diagram are timelines. A timeline typically represents a hardware or software tier. A rectangle on a timeline represents a time-consuming sequence of instructions being executed on that timeline's tier. Demand flows from left to right, and supply flows from right to left.

So, on my sequence diagram, the scheduler starts PYUGEN, which makes calls via Oracle network software called *SQL*Net* to its database. The diagram shows PYUGEN making only two database calls through SQL*Net, but the picture is meant to represent the roughly 100,000 round trips that we saw in our trace data.

A quick sketch of a sequence diagram like the one I've shown here can help you envision how a system spends your time. Being a little more careful—for example, scaling the heights of a diagram's rectangles in proportion to the time consumptions they represent—can provide additional insight about where your time is going. The information that allows you to do that comes from tracing.

18

The Gantt Chart

One of our clients had an overnight batch problem. They would kick off a big job every midnight to summarize the prior day's data and prepare the system for business at 8:00 a.m. But the job had been taking longer and longer, and now it was running until 8:30, through the end of its window. They were paying fines to their own customers, for not having their system ready by 8:00 sharp.

To understand how this complex collection of overnight processes was spending our client's time, we used a type of bar chart called a *Gantt chart*. Gantt charts help you see where you're wasting time. They are another tool for helping you *look at* the right *it*. On a Gantt chart, time flows from left to right. The bars of a Gantt chart represent work being done, and the connector lines represent dependencies.

In our Gantt chart, we tracked where the database had spent its time overnight. It contained several occurrences of a pattern that looked like this:

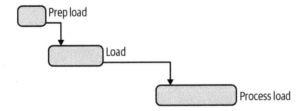

Seeing the process flow illustrated this way led several of us to ask, all at the same time, "What's happening in the time gap between loading and then processing that load? Why is the database not busy there?!" There was plenty of work to be done; why was the database not *doing* it? It's the question that cracked the case.

It turned out to be a performance improvement opportunity in the application, not the database. The solution had already been identified in a pile of recommendations that our client had intended to investigate one day, but nobody had suspected that this particular one mattered enough to require attention anytime soon. Of course, seeing it now as the direct impediment to their business's top-priority symptom meant that they would address it now, urgently.

Happily, attending to just this one pattern in a few places within the application was all they needed to cut more than three hours out of the job duration. Within a few days, they had their nightly batch jobs finishing by 5:00 a.m.

19

Tracing

All of the optimization stories I've told so far have motivated and remotivated the three-word prescription, *look at it*. In the Phyllis story, the *look at it* step came to me in the form of an unintentional ambush. In the Nancy case, looking at her screen as she typed was the key to understanding that she was unaware of a helpful feature. Likewise, all I needed in Orange County to see the label-printing symptom was a good tour guide and my own two eyes.

But in the order confirmation problem in Orange County and the payroll problem in Dallas, *looking at it* was more complicated than just seeing something physical. How do you "look at" how a computer program spends time? The answer is, you *trace* it.

Tracing creates a stream of output that explains the steps that your program is executing. Tracing can be a feature of the program you're diagnosing, or it can be a service provided by a separate program. In its simplest form, tracing is simply the execution of some extra print statements that write information to a file about the progress of the program being executed.

For example, a simple tracing feature for a procedure to process an invoice might look like this:

```
1.  procedure processInvoice(n) {
2.      if TRACING printf(TRC, "%s processInvoice(%d) {\n", now, n);
3.      // the work of processing invoice #n goes here
4.      if TRACING printf(TRC, "%s }\n", now);
5.  }
```

Then a program that processes many invoices inside of a loop would write trace data that looks like this:

```
1. ...
2. 2020-11-14T12:54:22.348127 processInvoice(99242) {
3. 2020-11-14T12:54:22.494281 }
4. 2020-11-14T12:54:22.741811 processInvoice(99243) {
5. 2020-11-14T12:54:23.019135 }
6. ...
```

From the data shown here, you could, for example, calculate the duration of each processInvoice call by subtracting the begin time of each call from its end time.

Tracing is a feature that the developer of any computer program can include or not, depending on what the specification requires (or what the programmer can sneak into the code to help themselves later when they have to debug it). It was Oracle Database instrumentation resembling these printf statements that helped Team 2 find the table lock in Orange County that was causing the problem with order confirmation numbers. And it's what we used in Dallas to solve the Payroll problem.

You can also trace programs without having to add extra instructions into the source code. eBPF, DTrace, strace, truss, tcpdump, and ETW are all tools that help you see what other people's programs are doing, whether they've included tracing features or not.

20

The Profile

A *profile* is a table that summarizes a trace stream by grouping on one or more of its attributes. It was a profile that helped us solve the Payroll problem:

Subroutine	Duration		Count	Mean
	seconds	%		
SQL*Net message from client	984.010	50.3%	95,161	0.010 340
SQL*Net more data from client	418.820	21.4%	3,345	0.125 208
db file sequential read	279.340	14.3%	45,084	0.006 196
12 other subroutines	275.300	14.1%	281,727	0.000 977
Total (15)	1,957.470	100.0%	425,317	0.004 602

In this profile, the grouping key is the subroutine name. Since most Oracle subroutine calls are associated with a "cursor" that has a SQL or PL/SQL statement attribute, you can also group Oracle trace data by statement:

Statement	Duration		Count	Mean
	seconds	%		
select ASSBAL.defined_bala…	627.900	32.1%	12,794	0.049 078
select ITEM_NAME,ITEM_…	278.500	14.2%	31,779	0.008 764
select fi.formula_name,fi.stic…	128.500	6.6%	12,621	0.010 181
270 other statements	922.570	47.1%	368,123	0.002 506
Total (273)	1,957.470	100.0%	425,317	0.004 602

In the Payroll story, the profile by subroutine was more useful to us than the profile by statement, but in other stories (see Richard's story later in the book for an example), the profile by statement is more useful. The important thing is that, no matter what you group by, the bottom line total duration—in this case, the 1,957.470 seconds for which we had traced PYUGEN—remains the same.

Of course, you can drill into just a part of a user's experience by filtering the trace data before you aggregate it. Here is a profile for just the 95,161 "SQL*Net message from client" calls in the trace data, grouped by statement:

Statement	Duration		Count	Mean
	seconds	%		
select ASSBAL.defined_bala...	562.540	57.2%	4,116	0.136 672
select fi.formula_name,fi.stic...	122.760	12.5%	2,647	0.046 377
select org_information5 into...	105.820	10.8%	20,128	0.005 257
142 other statements	192.890	19.6%	68,270	0.002 825
Total (145)	984.010	100.0%	95,161	0.010 340

You can group a profile by *any* attribute, including duration. For example, here is a profile of just the "SQL*Net message from client" calls, grouped by call duration ranges. Notice that the totals are the same as before. It's the same data, just viewed through a different dimension:

Call duration range	Duration		Count	Mean
	seconds	%		
recorded as 0.000	0.000	0.0%	75,988	0.000 000
between 0.010 and 0.099	248.280	25.2%	15,219	0.016 314
between 0.100 and 0.999	735.730	74.8%	3,954	0.186 072
Total (3)	984.010	100.0%	95,161	0.010 340

21

Creating a Profile

A profile is a tabular aggregation of a trace stream. It's a lot of detail, summarized in a form that's easy for a person to understand. To create a profile, your first step is to select the grouping key by which you want to aggregate. The aggregation is a mechanical process that I can illustrate with an example using a simple Microsoft Excel spreadsheet.

Imagine a tracing feature that records each execution of events called A, B, and C for a program that is important for you to *look at*. So then, every time your program executes an event, the event's name and duration are written to a trace file. Of course, in real life, you'd want a timestamp and some other attributes for each line, but I'll keep it simple for the example.

So, imagine that the resulting trace stream is stored in a spreadsheet, so that column A contains event names and column B contains durations, like this:

	A	B
1	Event	Duration
2	C	0.088
3	B	0.096
4	A	0.075
5	...	...

Let's say that you want to group this trace stream by event name. You could use the following Excel functions to create a *profile by event*:

	D	E	F	G
1	Event	Duration	Executions	Mean dur/exec
2	A	=SUMIF(A:A,D2,B:B)	=COUNTIF(A:A,D2)	=E2/F2
3	B	=SUMIF(A:A,D3,B:B)	=COUNTIF(A:A,D3)	=E3/F3
4	C	=SUMIF(A:A,D4,B:B)	=COUNTIF(A:A,D4)	=E4/F4
5	Total	=SUM(E2:E4)	=SUM(F2:F4)	=E5/F5

This is the kind of work that a profiler does for you. Of course, it's trickier than this in real life, where profilers have to cope with problems like:

Overlapping events
> When events nest, you can't just sum their durations. You have to devise a strategy for explaining parent–child relationships without double-counting.

Code coverage
> The events you trace will never cover all your program's code path. You have to devise a strategy for explaining the gaps.

Speed
> The profiler will need to be fast enough to process information about millions of event executions without taking too long.

The complexity of the aggregation process depends upon how carefully the tracing feature is designed. But if you need to answer questions about performance, then you need good trace data, and a good profiler. Profiling has taught me more about performance than anything else I've ever done.

PART IV

Measuring Performance

22

Performance Is a Feature

I've given a lot of presentations in which I say, "Performance is a feature." People nod when I say it, but I always go on to explain what I mean because the simple sentence doesn't completely convey the point that I want to get across. I think what most people think I'm saying is:

> *Going fast is important for a computer program, so you should design "going fast" into all your programs. You should treat "going fast" like a proper first-class feature, with specs and tests and everything.*

This interpretation is a start, but what I mean goes deeper.

Imagine if I were to ask a CTO of a company that sells things on the internet, "How many dollars worth of orders did your company book this month on your system? How does that compare to last month?" Just about any CTO would be able to find that information within a minute or two. Information about order volumes is probably easy to find in the application, because it's important to the business.

Now, imagine asking that same CTO, "How long did it take this month to book an order when people clicked the Book Order button? How does that compare to last month?" Many CTOs are not going to be able to tell you that. Is it important? Well, you decide. What if the answer would have been this:

> *Last month, 99.9% of Book Order clicks took 1.370 seconds or less, but this month we're at 2.799 seconds. That's not unacceptable (yet), but it has more than doubled in just one month.*

How would you rather find out that you have a creeping Book Order performance problem? By having your users call you because they're running out of patience? Or by having the system tell you before anyone else notices? You can make software do that. It's a feature.

If *performance* is important to the business, then *observability* about performance is important to the business. Observability is vital to great performance, because things that are easier to measure are easier to improve.

So, if performance is a feature that's important to you, then there should be a table somewhere on the system that you can query to find out how long everybody's Book Order and Payroll and Generate RMA features are taking. Maybe not for every feature in your application, but at least the most vital ones. You should be able to figure out (*before* you get a phone call about it) that in Atlanta, everybody's clicks go 20% slower than the same clicks executed in Phoenix.

Not only should you know about problems before your users do, you should be able to collect detailed data about why a program is acting up so that you can fix it—ideally, before anyone even notices a problem was brewing.[1] Getting the appropriate detail is a matter of tracing. Tracing is a key observability feature and, thus, a key performance feature.

How will you collect the data? How long will you retain it? How will you control what to trace? Will you trace everything and then discard what you don't want to retain? (That's what Google does; they keep the outliers in detail and discard much of the remainder.) Or will you trace only selected program executions?

Those—and many more—are all great questions that you'll discuss as you formally spec the new performance features you're thinking about.

---

1 The ideal time to fix such problems is before the application is ever released, when it is being designed and developed.

23

The Reproducible Test Case

Lately I've been having trouble with the software I'm using to write this book. It's the drop-down list box that lets me choose a character style for the characters I've selected. The way it's supposed to work is that when I click it, a list drops down, showing all my character styles. When I select one, that style is applied to my selection. But sometimes, it doesn't work. Sometimes, I click on the drop-down list box and my screen just flashes. The box doesn't open, so I can't apply the character style I want. I have to restart the application to make it work properly.

Of course, I've logged a bug. But I have virtually no hope that they'll ever fix it. At least not in response to *my* bug report. The reason is…the *sometimes*. I don't know how to reproduce it. I'd love to be able to say, "Just do these three steps, and you'll see the bug with the Character Style drop-down box, just like I'm seeing it." But I can't. The best I'd be able to say is, "Here are my book's 100+ document files. Have someone edit these files for a few hours until the Character Style drop-down box stops working."

So, what do you think the company that makes my software is going to do?

a. Play around with my 100+ document files on a system just like mine for a few hours until the Character Style drop-down box stops working.

b. Study all the aspects of their application code that might accidentally be causing the behavior I'm experiencing.

c. Push my bug report to the side and move on with the other bugs that they *can* reproduce and get rewarded for fixing.

All my available evidence suggests that the answer is *c*.

Whenever you find a problem, the best way to get someone to help you is to provide a *reproducible test case*, containing the following information:

1. How can someone reproduce your problem?
2. What did you expect to happen?
3. What happened instead?

You should log *all* defects this way, both functional defects *and* performance defects. If you can show me how I can reproduce your problem, I can study, experiment, and optimize. And when I've solved your problem, I can prove it:

> *Alright, here it is running for over ten minutes, just like you reported. So, let's kill that run, and let me show you the new version. Now it runs in just a shade less than five seconds, and the output's just like you want it, right? OK. Now, you try it.*

With a reproducible test case it's easier to help people:

- You can *look at* what the user is seeing.
- You can run the test case as often as you want while you're iterating through potential cures.
- You can *prove* the value of your solution. Ultimately, it's that *proof* that seals your success.

24

Intermittent Problems

Life is just easier when you have a reproducible test case. Nancy, for example, knew to tee up the Xerox bill for me to see. Phyllis knew just what to run to convince herself whether the system was sufficiently "faster enough" after this Oracle guy's disk rebalancing act. But what do you do when your problem is unpredictable, when you can't reproduce it every time?

We see it a lot. It's kind of ironic: you'd think a problem that happens only rarely would be less of a problem than one that happens all the time. But often the intermittent problems carry the highest business priority.

You can diagnose intermittent performance problems the same way convenience stores identify robbers: they leave the cameras running all the time. Likewise, you can trace every execution of a troublesome program until you can catch one in the act of misbehaving. Trace as much as you need, but as little as you can. If you can target just a particular feature that's misbehaving, then do that. If you can't, then trace just one program, or one application, or one user. Even if your software gives you lots of control over what you trace, sometimes you just have to trace everything.

There are two reasons you should trace the smallest scope you can:

- You don't want the trace itself to damage anyone's performance. A well-designed trace feature will incur as little *measurement intrusion effect* as possible. For example, in the Oracle world I've worked in for so long, the database's tracing feature is lightweight enough that you can trace a whole database without users noticing when it's enabled.

- When your trace is done, you're going to have to sift through all the trace data to find and then isolate the transactions that are misbehaving. This is easy if your *span* elements are defined to match your user's distinct experiences.[1] If they're not, then the sifting will be more difficult. The less data you have to look through, the faster and easier your job is going to be, even if you have good tools to help you.

Ideally, you'll trace enough workload that you'll catch all your interesting programs in the act of misbehaving. But it's not always easy. You might have to wait longer than you want for the misbehavior to recur. In the meantime, though, there are two great reasons to be tracing your programs when they're behaving nicely:

- Having a baseline to compare against will take a lot of pressure off your imagination when you eventually do catch a misbehaving execution. It is easy to hold two profiles side by side and see—aha!—*here* is where the extra time is being spent when this program misbehaves. It's a lot trickier to look at the profile of a misbehaving program and imagine what might have been different when it was finishing more quickly.

- You may be able to smell a scalability problem, even when the scalability problem is not creating a symptom for anyone. A program that is running inefficiently—even if it's fast—is especially susceptible to poor performance as the load on a system gets heavier.

---

1 OpenTelemetry, "OpenTracing," *https://oreil.ly/VGmKl*. Spans are the building blocks of traces in the OpenTelemetry standard.

25

How Much to Trace

You want your profile's bottom line to match the experience you're trying to observe. It wouldn't be good, for example, for your waiter to tell you your bill is $100 but then hand you a receipt for $20. You'd be left unable to explain 80% of your expenditure, which wouldn't bode well for your reimbursement aspirations.

Likewise, if you know that a user waited 100 minutes for an order confirmation number, then you don't want a profile that explains only 20 minutes. But in fact it might be enough….Which is good because it's not always possible to get exactly the trace data you want.

In the Payroll story, for example, we asked when our client would next be running PYUGEN so we could look at it. The answer was that we could look at it now, because it's already running. We could have insisted upon a "perfect" trace of a fresh new PYUGEN execution, but instead we enabled tracing for a PYUGEN process that was already running. And what we learned worked out just fine. (By the way: it's a highly desirable feature for your tracing function to allow you to trace a program without having to restart it.)

So, how much of a program's execution do you really need to trace? Not always the whole thing, as it turns out. Imagine a program that last month ran in ten minutes (0:10), but now it takes eight hours (8:00). Do you really need to trace the whole eight-hour execution to learn why it's not running in ten minutes anymore? You don't. If you know how long a program *should* run, then you don't need to trace any more than about three times that target duration.[1] You can trace the beginning of the program, its middle, or its end; it doesn't matter.

---

1 Using this "three times" rule will ensure that at least 66.6% of your profile will be wasted time.

So, for a program that runs for 8:00 but should run in 0:10, just trace about 0:30 of it. No matter which 0:30 of it you trace, you'll have at least 0:20 of wasteful work that shouldn't be in the profile. It'll be especially easy to spot if you have a baseline profile to show you how the program behaved when it used to run in 0:10. After you cure the cause of the 0:20 of waste, you'll have a program that finishes at least twenty minutes earlier than it did—and most likely even earlier than that.

These steps add detail to the *observe* step in Method R:

1. List the symptoms for which the business needs relief.
2. Sort the list into business-priority order.
3. For each symptom S in the sorted list:
4.   While further relief is required for symptom S:
5.   Observe S (*look at it!*), ideally, in the act of misbehaving.
6.   **Trace the program P that exhibits symptom S.**
7.   **If P has run for longer than 3 times its targeted duration:**
8.   **Disable the trace for P.**
9.   **Kill P if the business doesn't need it to finish.**
10.   Find the cause C of the misbehavior.
11.   Relieve S by curing C.

So, of course there's such a thing as "not enough trace data," but you don't necessarily need to have a whole execution's worth to be productive.

So then, is there such a thing as "*too much* trace data"? There is.

Imagine that you know your order confirmation feature takes 40 minutes for a user to run, but the profile you're looking at explains 300 minutes of execution time. Then you have some extra work to do, because your trace file filtration and aggregation process has failed you. You can't start chopping out waste that your profile points out, because the waste you see may be executed by something other than the order confirmation feature. You could theoretically cut up to 260 minutes of waste out of your profile and still never have touched the order confirmation feature (that has to be fixed before Friday or you'll die).

There are two solutions:

- Restrict your trace so that it contains only information about the interesting program executions that you're trying to *look at*. That is, don't trace what you don't want to see.

- If you can't restrict your trace the way you'd like, then restrict your profile to the subset of the trace that you want to look at. That is, crop your trace data as you would crop a photograph, to eliminate information that should be excluded from the analysis you're trying to focus on.

And if you see from your trace stream that several processes cooperate in parallel to accomplish your user's order confirmation feature? Then draw a Gantt chart and figure out which parts of your trace are on your critical path.

26

Identifying Experiences

In all my years of tracing Oracle, the hardest part has been knowing where in the trace stream the users' experiences begin and end. My colleague Jeff Holt and I have developed some tricks to figure it out, but the best way to know it is to have your software mark those events for you. Oracle has some good tools for doing it, but most application developers don't use them.

It's not enough just to make tools available to developers; those developers also have to have the will and the skill to use them. I'm optimistic, though, because I see good people working on the right problem. The OpenTelemetry standard, for example, has the right ingredients for accomplishing the goal of identifying individual user experiences.

27

Measurement
Intrusion

Once at a packed 5,000-person convention hall, my friend Tom Kyte answered a great question from the floor: "Tom, the Oracle Database has a lot of performance instrumentation built into it. It's always on, and so it's always using resources that my application could be using to go a little bit faster. How much overhead does all this instrumentation add to our response times?"

Tom thought for a few seconds, and then he answered, "Probably negative ten percent. Or less. Maybe even negative twenty or thirty percent."

He paused to give his now-vexed audience a moment to ponder what a negative percent was. Then he continued, "What I mean is that the database is at least ten percent *faster*—maybe even twenty or thirty percent—than it would have been without its instrumentation. Running that particular 'overhead' has helped our kernel developers make our database code faster and faster over time."

The performance penalty that a program endures when it measures itself is called *measurement intrusion effect*. Ideally, performance measurement should be so lightweight that its intrusion is unnoticeable. As it so happens, people are accustomed to response time fluctuations of ±5% or so from their programs anyway,[1,2] so if tracing costs less than 5%, people tend not to notice it.

But tracing doesn't have to be unnoticeable to be valuable. Even if tracing were to cause a one-hour program to take two hours—if a trace teaches you how to make that one-hour program run in half the time, then you'll save 500 hours of user experience

---

1 You can see for yourself: just time a few executions of a simple file copy command.

2 Millsap, *Mastering Oracle Trace Data*.

duration over the course of that program's next 1,000 executions. Not a bad payback on a one-time, one-hour investment.

The trade-offs of tracing are rarely as bad as people fear. Well-designed tracing can be both rich and lightweight. Oracle is proof that it's possible. Since 1992, their tracing feature has been rich enough to serve as a primary performance data source, and it's lightweight enough that, if you do it right, you can trace everything on a huge system for hours at a time without anyone noticing.[3]

Oracle provides three tracing features that give analysts the control they need in the battle between information richness and measurement intrusion:

Session targeting
> You can trace all of a system's users if you want to, or just individuals or groups of users if you prefer.

Aspect targeting
> You can trace different aspects of the system: for example, database and system calls, cache manipulations, or sort operations.

Adjustable levels
> You can decide how much detail you want; for example, with database and system call tracing, you can adjust whether to see details about how values are bound to statement placeholders.

These are great features worth mimicking in whatever systems you're running, building, or imagining today.

---

3 Nils-Peter Nelson in Jon Bentley, *More Programming Pearls: Confessions of a Coder* (Reading, MA: Addison-Wesley Professional, 1988), 62.

PART V

Optimizing

A Riddle

Riddles are fun. Here's a riddle for you:

There are only two ways to improve the response time of a computer program. What are they?

People usually guess answers like these:

- CPU, disk, network? Oh, wait, that's three…
- User calls and system calls?
- Service time and queueing delay?
- Queueing delay and coherency delay?

Those are interesting answers, and I discuss them all in this book. But they're not the answer I'm looking for. Like with many riddles, the answer is probably hiding in a different dimension than you're thinking of.

Let's go back to the receipt metaphor for a moment. Imagine you sent your fifteen-year-old son into the grocery store with your credit card for tomatoes while you waited in the car. He returns with a suspiciously full-looking bag.

"How much was it?" you ask, and he responds, "About fifty bucks." You're thinking, whoa, $50 is way too much for a few tomatoes. It's a problem. "Hand me the receipt," you say. You could have looked in the bag, but the receipt is actually more informative, because they don't put price tags on groceries anymore.

Here's what it says:

```
SCHOGETTEN CHOC
20 @ $2.00 EA              $40.00
VINE RIPE TOMATO
1.20 lb @ $12.90 / lb     $15.48

SUB TOTAL                 $55.48

TOTAL                     $55.48
```

Aw, you should have known. Look at the biggest contributor to the total price: he snuck in a bunch of those chocolate bars he likes. Twenty of them. It's a running joke now. It's his "chocolate tax" that he charges for running into the store for you. But he already has plenty at home. Returning the chocolate bars will save $40, which will leave $15.48. That's a good first step.

There's a second issue: they got the price wrong for the tomatoes. The numbers look right, but not the decimal point. The price should be $1.29 per pound, not $12.90. (You have to know something about tomatoes to know that.) Fixing that will drop the receipt total to 1.20 lb × $1.29/lb = $1.55.

That's more like it. A quick trip to the Customer Service desk seals the deal.

In this story, you've used two techniques to reduce your bill by more than 97%: (1) you've reduced a quantity and (2) you've reduced a price. These are in fact the *only* two ways you can reduce a receipt total. These two techniques are not only all you have, they're all you need. They work no matter what you're buying, whether it's tomatoes and chocolate bars, or trisodium phosphate and puppies, or even network calls and CPU cycles. Anything that has a quantity and a price.

Let's look at the profile for PYUGEN again, in its receipt-like form:

Subroutine	Duration		Count	Mean
	seconds	%		
SQL*Net message from client	984.010	50.3%	95,161	0.010 340
SQL*Net more data from client	418.820	21.4%	3,345	0.125 208
db file sequential read	279.340	14.3%	45,084	0.006 196
12 other subroutines	275.300	14.1%	281,727	0.000 977
Total (15)	1,957.470	100.0%	425,317	0.004 602

In this table, *duration* = *count* × *mean*. Clearly, there are only two ways to reduce a duration:

1. Reduce a count, or

2. Reduce a mean.

This, of course, is the solution to the riddle.

The beauty of the riddle is its *only*: there are *only* two ways to reduce the response time of a computer program. It means that arranging your performance data into the receipt-style profile format liberates you from having to understand thousands of possible causes that *might* have made your program slow. It means that, to know exactly why your business's highest-priority symptom consumes the time it does, all you have to understand is the handful of event types that *did* make your program slow.

A profile shows how a program spent its time.
It also shows how it didn't.

29

A Game

There are only two ways to improve the response time of a computer program: (1) reduce a profile component's event count or (2) reduce a profile component's mean duration per event. It's true. An interesting game to fortify your confidence about it is to recast your old performance improvement stories into this new "quantity or price" way of thinking.

To play the game, you describe a performance fix you've implemented or heard about, and then the class explains the differences you'd have seen in the *before* and *after* profiles of the symptoms you relieved. Like this:

> *Phyllis's report sped up when I balanced her files across more disk drives.*

Spreading files across more drives probably reduced the I/O rate to each drive, which would have reduced the duration that each read or write request spent queueing for service. So after the change, her program probably had the same number of read and write calls as before, but the mean duration per call was probably smaller.

Here are some others for you to practice on. Can you explain, in terms of event counts and durations, how each of these fixes would have made a program go faster?

- "We removed another program's lock on the sales order table."
- "We installed faster CPUs."
- "We replaced a heapsort with a quicksort."
- "We indexed a database table."
- "We parallelized the part of the code that works on eight independent tables."
- "We allocated more memory to the database buffer cache."

Usually when I play this game with students, someone will claim, "I fixed something once, but you wouldn't be able to see it in any profile." This statement translates literally to, "I made an improvement that did not change the response time of any program on the system." This kind of claim opens the door to investigating the definition of the word "improvement." If a change doesn't make any program's response time better, then is the change really an improvement?

It *is* a question worth considering. For example, maybe the change has made the system less expensive to own or to operate. Maybe the change has made the system more reliable. Maybe it has increased your throughput. These are all good things that, certainly, I would call improvements. But if a change is destined not to improve any profiles, then it is destined not to improve anyone's response time.

The best way to play this game is to graduate from thought experiments to real experiments. Trace your high-priority programs before and after a change whose effect you want to measure, and compare your profiles. This is the fastest way I know to get smart about performance.

30

Event Count

There are only two ways to improve the response time of a computer program: (1) reduce a profile component's event count or (2) reduce a profile component's mean duration per event. In this chapter, I will tell you about the first way: reducing event counts.

In the tomato story I told earlier, eliminating the chocolate bars saved $40.00 of a $55.48 grocery bill:

Baseline...

```
SCHOGETTEN CHOC
20 @ $2.00 EA            $40.00
VINE RIPE TOMATO
1.20 lb @ $12.90 / lb   $15.48

SUB TOTAL               $55.48

TOTAL                   $55.48
```

20 chocolate bars eliminated...

```
VINE RIPE TOMATO
1.20 lb @ $12.90 / lb   $15.48

SUB TOTAL               $15.48

TOTAL                   $15.48
```

You'll see the same kinds of opportunities in the receipt-style profile of a computer program. Opportunities to reduce event counts can occur anywhere from Nancy's brain all the way down to your computer's silicon. That's because everyone who has ever played a part in designing, building, configuring, managing, or using your system has had countless opportunities to accidentally add waste to your system. Our job is to recognize the waste that matters and get rid of it.

So, programs execute lots of events. How can you tell the *wasteful* ones from the *necessary* ones? Sometimes it's as easy as the chocolate bar question. If you don't need a feature, then turn it off! Others, you just have to learn. You'll learn from blogs and papers and conferences, and books and courses and your own experiences, and friends and colleagues and vendors, and from tests you do yourself.

You can fast-track your progress by tracing important application tasks when they're running at speeds that everyone is satisfied with. That way, when a task starts behaving badly, you'll have a baseline to tell you what *normal* looks like. It's much easier to see waste when you can hold the profile of a bad execution side by side with the profile of a good one.

Eliminating unnecessary events helps you in two ways. The primary benefit is obvious: a process that executes fewer instructions usually consumes less time. But there is collateral benefit as well. By reducing event counts in one program, you free up resources that other programs can use without having to wait so long. It is especially helpful, systemwide, to reduce call counts in programs that are executed by lots of users simultaneously.

Of course, reducing an event count to zero—entirely eliminating its row from the profile—is the ultimate optimization for a given event type. It's what you get when you take back *all* the chocolate bars. It's what Team 2 did in Orange County when they reduced the number of "wait for table lock" instructions to zero for the book-order process.

The fastest call is no call.[1]

---

1 Nils-Peter Nelson in Bentley, *More Programming Pearls: Confessions of a Coder* (Reading, MA: Addison-Wesley Professional, 1988), 62.

31

Event Duration

Remember, there are only two ways to improve the response time of a computer program: (1) reduce a profile component's event count or (2) reduce a profile component's mean duration per event. In this chapter, I will tell you about the second way: reducing the duration.

In the tomato story I told earlier, you had to know something about the price of tomatoes—specifically, that $12.90 per pound was absurd—to make the final optimization to that shopping trip:

Baseline...

20 chocolate bars eliminated, price of tomatoes adjusted...

```
SCHOGETTEN CHOC
20 @ $2.00 EA          $40.00
VINE RIPE TOMATO
1.20 lb @ $12.90 / lb  $15.48

SUB TOTAL             $55.48

TOTAL                $55.48
```

```
VINE RIPE TOMATO
1.20 lb @ $1.29 / lb   $1.55

SUB TOTAL              $1.55

TOTAL                 $1.55
```

It's like that with computer optimization, too. The Payroll story is a good example. Jeff "knew the price of tomatoes" in that engagement. He recognized that a network round-trip duration of 10 milliseconds was excessive for two processes running on the same computer. At the time, I didn't know how much a network round trip like that was supposed to cost. Would you?

Since that day, I've wondered out loud whether I'd have ever found the problem had Jeff not been there. Jeff argues, charitably, that I would have. He's probably right. The profile proved that the only way to make PYUGEN meaningfully faster was to improve either the "SQL*Net" call counts or their durations. Changing the round-trip call counts was not an option because it was Oracle's code, and we had no way to change it.

But that's OK. The call counts probably weren't a problem, because Payroll users at other companies weren't complaining. I would have been led forcibly by the data to the realization that the only possible cure was to improve the call durations. The profile would have confined my attention so tightly that finding the configuration mistake was probably inevitable.

When we got back to the office from that visit, Jeff and I created a little reference list of reasonable expectations for the Oracle events we encountered most commonly. In the early 2000s, we only needed five elements:[1]

- Oracle Database buffer cache access
- Single-block hard disk drive (HDD) read
- Network round trip via wide area network (WAN)
- Network round trip via local area network (LAN)
- Round trip via interprocess communication (IPC)

A more modern list would contain elements such as reads and writes on solid state drives (SSD) and network round trips on InfiniBand. Tomorrow's lists will contain elements that we wouldn't think of today. Where do you get the numbers? From the specs of the technology you've purchased. And they'll change over time, so you'll need to keep yourself updated.[2]

Once you know the maximum duration you should tolerate for a given event, you can tell right away when there's potential for improvement. What makes an event execution take longer than that maximum tolerable duration? The answer will be some combination of the following factors:

Work quantity

An event duration can vary in response to how much work the event does. For example, maybe it takes twice as long to post to your general ledger this year because your sales have doubled.

---

1 Millsap and Holt, *Optimizing Oracle Performance*, 295–296.

2 I just hope that tomatoes don't cost $12.90 a pound by the time you read this book.

Subevents

Just about any instrumented event can be thought of as a sequence of subevents. For example, in the Payroll story, each network round trip looked like a duration problem, but you could also view it as a call count problem deep down in the TCP/IP code stack.

Queueing delay

As a system gets busier, more processes have to queue for resources. Queueing is how, for example, your 2-millisecond call becomes a 10-millisecond call: that's 2 milliseconds for each of the four processes that your call waited behind in the queue, plus 2 milliseconds for you.

Coherency delay

Some processes depend on point-to-point communication with other processes. For example, two processes in a distributed database system may have to coordinate with each other to update a database buffer. The extra code it takes to do this coordination takes extra time to run.

Hardware errors

Sometimes the winner of the day is the hardware administrator who walks into the room with a big smile and the news that one of the network cables wasn't connected properly, and that's why some of your network I/O calls had been taking ten times longer than they should.

32

Filter Early

Have you ever moved? I mean, packed up all your stuff, put it in a truck, and driven it halfway across the country? Seems like every time I've done it, I spend time in my new place throwing stuff away as I unpack it. It's crazy. If I had just thrown that stuff away before I moved it, I could have bought fewer boxes and saved time packing and unpacking. Maybe I could have rented a smaller truck.

That's what happened to Nancy. She had been transporting every name in her company's vendor table across town and throwing away everything that wasn't Xerox. All this time, the guys in a room a few miles away were scratching their heads, wondering if they needed a bigger truck.

To *filter early* is to discard unwanted material as early in a process as possible. Whenever I see someone like Jeff make a database query run 100,000 times faster, it's almost always because he improved the data access algorithm to filter earlier. Here's an example of how he does it. Here's before:

1. *# Baseline: algorithm is slow because it filters late*
2. For each row R (1,000,000 rows):
3.   Calculate some result $S = f(R)$.
4.   If R matches our predicate (10 rows), then add S to the result set.

And here's after:

1. *# After improving: algorithm is 100,000× faster because it filters early*
2. For each row R that matches our predicate (10 rows):
3.   Add $S = f(R)$ to the result set.

The baseline algorithm will execute f a million times. The improved algorithm will execute f ten times. If f consumes just 0.000 500 seconds per call, then the baseline algorithm will consume 500 seconds (over 8 minutes), but the improved algorithm will consume only 0.005 seconds. It's literally 100,000 times faster.[1] Of course, an improvement like this can make a huge difference for a business, especially if the program is run frequently by a lot of users.

It sounds crazy, but we see filter-late code all the time. It's usually not because the people who wrote it were dumb; most often they've written code that accidentally filters later because their application execution details are difficult to observe. Like, for instance, if they don't have a tracing feature.

Filtering early is why databases have indexes. A database index works kind of like the index in this book: if you're looking for discussion of "Payroll," the fastest way to find it is through the list of page numbers in the "Payroll" index entry. The index helps you skip pages that don't discuss "Payroll."

But an index wouldn't be as useful for some other words. For example, using an index to find the word "the" would be a terrible idea. A "the" index entry would list nearly every page in the book, which wouldn't save you any time at all. You'd be better off just reading the whole book without flipping back and forth to the index, occasionally skipping a page.

Deciding when to use an index is more complicated than you might have expected. For example, if all the words in the whole book were on just one page (little words on big pages), then an index would be useless, even for finding "Payroll." But if there were only one word per page (big words on little pages), then an index would be useful even for words like "the." Navigating trade-offs like this is one of the reasons people who can optimize might get paid a little more than your average bear.

---

1 ((1,000,000 rows) × (0.000 500 seconds/row)) / ((10 rows) × (0.000 500 seconds/row)) = 100,000.

33

Look Left

This happens a lot:

> *We're seeing heavy consumption of x, but our x administrator tells us that our x is performing great.*

The poor x administrator is in the corner of the meeting room, periodically interjecting truthful statistics that show he's not the problem, as debate rages. There's even a saying around the company: "It's always the x." You know that other companies have the same saying, because when you say it at a conference, everybody laughs.

Here's what I encourage you to do. First, make sure you're *looking at* the right *it*. Something has happened in these people's past to make them incriminate x as their highest priority problem. But x doesn't have a priority on its own, because it's not a *symptom*, only a *cause*—and only a *potential* cause at that. The only priority a cause can have is the priority of the symptom it creates. So, find out what the real symptom is that they're worried about.

Here's a secret. No businessperson cares about their x, unless:

a. That person believes that the only way to get technical people to listen is to try to "speak their language."

b. There's an unsubstantiated belief that x causes an important symptom.

c. There's a substantiated belief that x causes an important symptom.

The only legitimate reason to care about x is c: "There's a substantiated belief that x causes an important symptom." You shouldn't worry about x until the trace of an important symptom implicates x as a cause (current or future). Once you've implicated x, there are only two ways that x can be causing a problem for your program: call counts, or call durations.

- If your call count is too high, then you don't have a problem with x, you have a problem with the programs that are calling x. Your problem is left of the x tier in your sequence diagram.

- If your durations are out of bounds, then it's either because of queueing or because of errors:

  — If it's queueing, then it's not a problem with x; it's a problem with the programs that are calling x, left of the x tier in your sequence diagram.

  — If it's errors (configuration parameters, poor cable connections, failing devices…), then you need your x administrator to figure it out.

In the errors case, it's your x administrator's problem. In all other cases, it's not helpful—or fair—to say that x is your problem.

Look left is just another way of saying *filter early*. The farther left in a sequence diagram you can eliminate events, the more leverage you can have. Take Nancy's case for example. Remember, Nancy and her teammates were paging through 27 pages of vendor data, looking for Xerox, while the poor administrators were trying to figure out what to do about the disk and network being so busy.

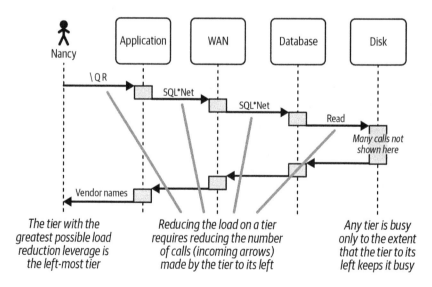

The tier with the greatest possible load reduction leverage is the left-most tier

Reducing the load on a tier requires reducing the number of calls (incoming arrows) made by the tier to its left

Any tier is busy only to the extent that the tier to its left keeps it busy

We could have bought faster disks. Or faster CPUs for the database. Or a faster network. Or we could have made the application fetch more database rows per network round trip. But none of that would have been as effective as teaching Nancy how to find Xerox without having to filter through all the vendor names herself.

While you're looking for calls to eliminate, don't stop at the caller. Look left even farther, at the caller's caller, and the caller's caller's caller. Look left all the way to where the user is. Ask whether apparent requirements are really legitimate requirements. There's no more efficient way to reduce load than to realize, hey, we don't actually even need to *run* that. Nancy can tell you. So can Debra.

Filter early, every way you can, as far left in the sequence diagram as you can go.

34

Tow–Millsap Law

My friend Dan Tow and I once had a dinner conversation that led to the following postulate:[1]

No human ever wants to see more than ten rows
(Tow–Millsap law).

Our idea was that once you're presented with more than ten rows to look at, you'd really rather see some kind of aggregation of the data instead (count, sum, average, a graph…). Or, in Nancy's case, just the one vendor name she was looking for instead of 800 that she never wanted to see in the first place.

So, the next time you're asked to improve the performance of a program that returns a bazillion rows, at least ask whether the user using your program really wants to see all bazillion of them. It's easier, cheaper, and more effective to give a user less data—only what she really wants—than to make your program faster at returning stuff that people didn't really want to begin with.

---

1 Dan Tow, a former colleague from my years at Oracle Corporation, is the author of *SQL Tuning: Generating Optimal Execution Plans* (O'Reilly, 2003).

35

The Bottleneck

Maybe you've heard that performance is all about eliminating bottlenecks. The word itself is a metaphor: it doesn't matter how big the bottle's body is, the amount you can get out of it in a given time interval is constricted by the size of the little opening there at the end.

Stories about bottles and water pipes and such are fine for learning principles, but they don't tell you what to type. And it so happens that you have to be careful about how you define *bottleneck* for the principle to be helpful. Here's the definition you need: the resource that dominates the response time for a task execution is that execution's *bottleneck*. If you have a profile for the execution you're observing, then the definition is even simpler:

The bottleneck for a program execution is that execution's largest response time contributor.

Let's try it out. In the Payroll story, what's the bottleneck of the PYUGEN execution? Here's the profile again, to jog your memory:

Subroutine	Duration		Count	Mean
	seconds	%		
SQL*Net message from client	984.010	50.3%	95,161	0.010 340
SQL*Net more data from client	418.820	21.4%	3,345	0.125 208
db file sequential read	279.340	14.3%	45,084	0.006 196
CPU service, EXEC calls	136.880	7.0%	67,888	0.002 016
CPU service, PARSE calls	74.490	3.8%	10,098	0.007 377
CPU service, FETCH calls	37.320	1.9%	57,217	0.000 652
latch free	23.690	1.2%	34,695	0.000 683
8 other subroutines	2.920	0.1%	111,829	0.000 026
Total (15)	1,957.470	100.0%	425,317	0.004 602

Since the profile is sorted in descending order of duration, the bottleneck is the subroutine listed in the first line of the body: it's "SQL*Net message from client." This root cause offers the biggest opportunity for improvement, because that's where most of PYUGEN's time is being spent.

Amdahl's law restricts your performance improvement opportunity to the proportion of how much your program uses the thing you want to improve.[1] For example, if you reduced your "db file sequential read" time by 90%, you'd improve PYUGEN performance by only 90% × 14.3% ≈ 13%. But if you reduced your "SQL*Net message from client" time by even just 50%, you'd improve PYUGEN by 50% × 50.3% ≈ 25%.

---

1 "Amdahl's law," Wikipedia, *https://oreil.ly/e9YGD*.

36

Beware the "System Bottleneck"

Not everyone defines *bottleneck* as an attribute of a program execution. A popular alternative definition of bottleneck that people use is: a *system's* bottleneck is the resource at which the system spends the most time. Let's play with that definition for a moment.

Recall in the Payroll story that the systemwide monitoring tools had shown that the system's top two bottlenecks were (1) CPU and (2) "latch free." But observe these alleged "bottlenecks" in the PYUGEN profile. If you were to eliminate its need for CPU consumption altogether (which you can't), you'd make only a 12.7% difference.[1] If you were to eliminate latches from the face of the Earth, you'd make only an imperceptible 1.2% difference.

Looking at their system's bottleneck instead of their high-priority program's bottleneck earned our customer months of frustration, a bunch of torn-up office buildings, and a profound sense of confusion after an expensive CPU upgrade made their most important program even slower than it was before.

The moral of this story:

Don't take your eye off your real goal.

I understand that you want to optimize your whole system, but the best way to do it is one prioritized *symptom* at a time. Looking at systemwide aggregated statistics can take you way off your optimal path. To stay relevant, look at the bottleneck for your business's highest priority symptom.

---

1 $(7.0 + 3.8 + 1.9)\% = 12.7\%$.

37

The Problem with Optimizing Subsystems

Contrary to what might sound like common sense, you cannot optimize a system by optimizing each of its components in isolation. Troubles often hide in the interrelationships among a system's components. Here's a story of how looking at component metrics can cause you to lose attention on the overall goal you're trying to achieve.

Patty wants to go to a conference. Here is her approved travel expense proposal. Each line item fits within the constraints documented in the Employee Handbook. Could you optimize it?

Conference expenses	Amount	Description
Airfare	$1,250	Airfare to/from conference city
Ground transportation	$60	2 taxi home/airport @ $30/ride
Rental car	$280	4 days @ $70/day
Hotel parking	$100	4 days @ $25/day
Conference parking	$100	4 days @ $25/day
Hotel	$540	4 nights @ $135/night
Meals, partial-day	$92	2 days @ $46/day
Meals, full-day	$122	2 days @ $61/day
Total	$2,544	

The first thing I see is perhaps using a ride-share company instead of renting a car and paying for all the parking.

Conference expenses	Amount	Description
Airfare	$1,250	Airfare to/from conference city
Ground transportation	$60	2 taxi home/airport @ $30/ride
~~Rental car~~	~~$280~~	~~4 days @ $70/day~~
~~Hotel parking~~	~~$100~~	~~4 days @ $25/day~~
~~Conference parking~~	~~$100~~	~~4 days @ $25/day~~
Uber	$240	4 days @ $60/day
Hotel	$540	4 nights @ $135/night
Meals, partial-day	$92	2 days @ $46/day
Meals, full-day	$122	2 days @ $61/day
Total	$2,304	

That's a pretty good idea. It saved $240.

Note that adding the Uber line didn't just change one line in the proposal—it replaced *three*. This is because paying for a rental car and paying for parking are interdependent. Changing one can change the other.

So how about now: do you see any more optimization opportunities?

Another optimization, for both Patty's company and Patty herself, is to realize that if she books a room at the conference hotel (which has a free airport shuttle), she won't even need Uber, *and* she won't waste any of her time transiting to and from the conference hotel. Staying at the conference hotel means she'll be able to spend more time with the people her company is paying for her to go see. It's also safer for Patty, because every minute spent sitting in a car is a risk, and who knows what kind of a neighborhood it is that has a $135 hotel.

The problem is, the conference hotel costs $165/night, so the company policy prohibits her from staying there. The policy allows a maximum of only $135/night for hotel stays. But look what happens to the cost of her trip if you allow the policy violation:

Conference expenses	Amount	Description
Airfare	$1,250	Airfare to/from conference city
Ground transportation	$60	2 taxi home/airport @ $30/ride
~~Uber~~	~~$240~~	~~4 days @ $60/day~~
~~Hotel~~	~~$540~~	~~4 nights @ $135/night~~
Hotel	$660	4 nights @ $165/night
Meals, partial-day	$92	2 days @ $46/day
Meals, full-day	$122	2 days @ $61/day
Total	$2,184	

This proposal costs $360 less than the original approved one, and it yields a better experience. Both benefits are made possible by looking at the overall experience instead of a line-by-line analysis of Patty's proposal. It works the same with profiles of program executions. The trick is to recognize the interdependencies among the lines in the proposal. But to do this, you have to understand what your instrumented events mean.

It's just one more story that leads you to my central thesis in this book:

Look at it. The right it.

Look at the user experiences the system is creating, not just isolated metrics about your system's internals.

38

Every Problem Is a Skew Problem

I'm pretty sure that every performance problem I've ever helped solve can be framed as a skew problem. Even the label printer in Orange County. *Skew* is a nonuniformity in a list. It's everywhere:

- Do all your task executions have uniform priority? No, some are more important than others. This is skew in program priorities. The principal motivation for creating Method R is that the skew in your diagnostic priorities needs to match the skew in your business priorities.

- Do all the programs on a system have the same profile? No, different programs usually have different profiles. For example, PYUGEN spent more time doing network I/O than anything else, but other programs on the same system spent more time using CPU and waiting for latches than anything else.

- Do all event types contribute uniformly to a profile? No, usually, some event types contribute more to total duration than others. You'll probably never see a profile for a computer program with perfectly uniform contributions from all its event types.

- Do all the events of a given type contribute uniformly to a profile? No, some event executions take longer than other executions of the same event type. For example, your slowest hundred thousand disk read calls can contribute 100 times more duration than your fastest nine million calls.

- Does every execution of the same program have the same profile? No, a program might spend most of its time in the morning reading from SSD, and it might spend most of its time in the evening using CPU.

- Does your FTP server have 100% uptime? No, sometimes it's not running when it's supposed to be. This is skew in the status of the machine that's on the critical path for printing shipping labels.

Skew is *everywhere*. Some lines of code take longer than others. Some loop iterations take longer than others. Some tasks execute faster in *this* city than they do in *that* city. Some programs take longer at certain times of the day. It's just everywhere.

Finding skew is vital. When it's hiding from you, it makes predicting results more difficult, which in turn makes deciding what to do next more difficult. Skew was exactly the problem in the Payroll story. In the months before Jeff and I had been invited to help, the team there had viewed their system through the lens of statistics that were aggregated at the system level by an expensive tool. This is what their "system" had looked like, through the lens of that tool:

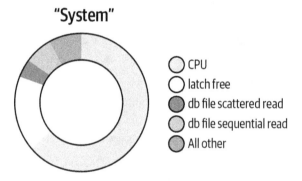

This view promoted an assumption that, since CPU was the system's bottleneck, therefore, CPU must be Payroll's bottleneck, too. And Book Order's, and Pick Order's, and Ship Order's, and everything else's as well.

Their worldview looked like this:

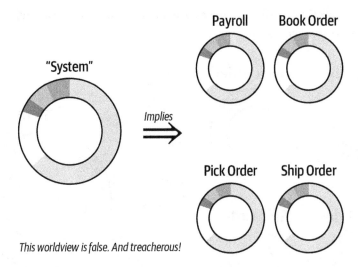

This worldview is false. And treacherous!

But the implication depicted here is *false!* You can *not* assume that every program on your system uses resources in the same proportions as your systemwide average. There will almost certainly be (1) skew among your programs' profiles and (2) skew in how much workload each program contributes, so there is no implication arrow going from your *system* view to your *symptom* view.

The *real* implication works only in the opposite direction, like this, with donut sizes drawn proportional to workload contribution. For example, even though the Payroll program is important to the business, its donut is small because Payroll represents only a small proportion of the system's overall workload.

Therefore, its profile of response time consumption by call type doesn't influence the systemwide average very much:

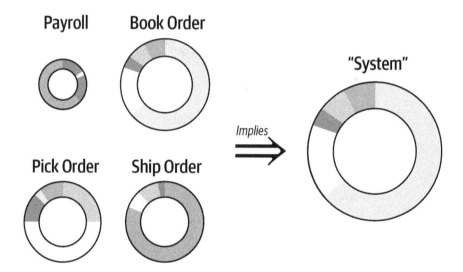

The truth that we found by tracing Payroll was that its execution profile looked virtually nothing like the overall system's aggregated "profile." First, its SQL*Net call dominance bore no resemblance to the system's apparent CPU and latch dominance. And second, Payroll's contribution to the overall system workload was so small that it didn't influence the systemwide data enough to alert anybody that its problems were important.

Skew is your story's villain if it's hiding from you. But once you find it, skew is your faithful servant. After all, skew is leverage—through Amdahl's law. For example, which of these two profiles would you rather see?

Event	Contribution	Event	Contribution
A	90	A	34
B	5	B	33
Other	5	Other	33
Total	100	Total	100

I'd rather see the skewed profile on the left than the uniform profile on the right. With the skewed profile, I might eliminate up to 90 units of time just by studying one event. But with the uniform profile, eliminating 90 units of time is going to require work on A *and* B *and* other events.

This is why you should always hunt the view of your trace data that presents the most skew. It's why you want your profiler to have different grouping keys. For example, in the Payroll case, the skew is in the profile grouped by subroutine call. In Richard's story (later in the book), the skew is in the profile grouped by SQL statement.

The high-skew view is the right view for you.

39

Critical Path

Here's a Gantt chart that depicts the execution of three tasks:

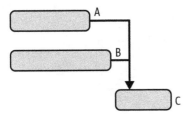

Tasks A and B can execute in parallel, and task C can't begin until both A and B are finished. The highest-priority symptom for this business is to get C to finish earlier. So, quick quiz: how much earlier would C finish if you could make A finish twice as quickly (that is, in half the time) as it does now?

Well, if A and B execute independently, then improving the speed of A won't make C finish any earlier at all:

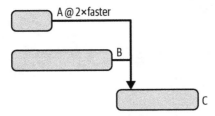

A Gantt chart analyst would say that improving the duration of A will not change the time at which C completes. This is because A is not on the sequence of tasks determining the minimum time needed for an operation, called the *critical path*.

And it makes sense. If A and B are independent,[1] then the only way to make C finish earlier is to reduce the duration of either B, or C itself. If you improve B so much that it runs in less time than A, then A will replace B on the critical path and become the focus of your attention. Understanding your critical path helps you make sure you're always working on the right problem.

---

1 The assumption that A and B execute independently may or may not be realistic. Imagine, for example, that B uses a lot of a resource for which A creates strenuous competition. Then reducing the duration of A might collaterally reduce the duration of B. The independence assumption I'm making here is thus similar to how a physics professor might begin an argument with a proposition like, "Assume a spherical cow of uniform density…" See "Spherical cow," Wikipedia, *https://oreil.ly/XROPx*.

PART VI

Delays

40

Kevin

Kevin's team was having trouble with a number of application features. Invoicing was at the top of his list. At his company's web page, a customer could click to create an up-to-date invoice. On a good day, this online feature would create an invoice in about 40 seconds. Kevin's team had never loved this level of performance, but it was their normal, and it was considered officially acceptable.

The problem was, over the span of a calendar month, this invoicing feature (and many others as well) would get slower and slower. By month-end, creating an invoice might take *300 seconds* or more, which was intolerable.

Kevin invited us to look at his system in early December, so it would be a few weeks before we'd have a chance to catch an invoice creation in the act of being slow. But of course, we wouldn't need to wait until month-end to trace a Create Invoice execution. Even if we couldn't yet catch it in the act of running slowly, tracing early in the month would help in at least three ways:

Setting a baseline
> Solving problems is easier if you can understand how the program you're analyzing behaves when you're happy with it.

Revealing waste
> A profile shows whether a program is wasting any of its time. (Being fast doesn't automatically imply being efficient.)

Starting the learning curve
> If you're not yet intimate with tracing, it's better to learn how to do it now, while everything's still calm.

Here's the profile for a typical execution. This one took about 41 seconds:

Subroutine	Duration	Count	Mean
block read	37.999	**81,964**	**0.000 464**
other	3.488	144	0.024 225
Total	**41.488**	82,108	0.000 505

The number that caught our attention first was the mean "block read" call duration. Reading a block from a secondary storage device (SSD in this case) in 0.000 464 seconds is *fast*. But there were so many calls (81,964 of them) that even with these super-fast reads, the invoice program was spending 38 seconds reading.

Even without seeing a misbehaving execution, you can smell a potential scalability problem just by wondering about an obvious *what-if* question: "What would happen if these amazing 0.000 464-second read calls were to degrade to some more unremarkable response time?" You don't have to wait for more data to know the answer. The profile has everything you need.

To answer the question, imagine the profile as a spreadsheet. The numbers within the C2:D3 box come from the profile. Everything else is calculated:

	A	B	C	D
1	Subroutine	Duration	Count	Mean
2	block read	=C2*D2	81964	.000464
3	other	=C3*D3	144	.024225
4	Total	=SUM(B2:B3)	=SUM(C2:C3)	=B4/C4

The numbers you enter in cells C2 and D2 determine the total "block read" duration in B2, which affects the total response time in B4. You can simulate a busy I/O subsystem that's making people wait for service by increasing the value of the mean call duration in D2.

Setting the mean call duration in D2 to 0.001 seconds, for example, yields:

Subroutine	Duration	Count	Mean
block read	**81.964**	81,964	**0.001 000**
other	3.488	144	0.024 225
Total	**85.452**	82,108	0.001 041

Noodling around with the spreadsheet shows the effect of degraded "block read" durations upon the overall performance of creating an invoice:

Mean "block read" duration	Create Invoice duration
0.000 464	41
0.001 000	85
0.002 167	167
0.004 000	331

The idea you should take from the profile spreadsheet is that, because "block read" is such a big proportion of total response time, changes in "block read" durations are going to have a big impact upon how long it takes to create an invoice. It's Amdahl's law.

Here's an interesting party trick: if your system administrators told you that "block read" response times were averaging 0.001 seconds, then it's a good guess that generating an invoice is taking at least 85 seconds. Approaching it from the other direction, if your users told you that generating an invoice was taking about five minutes (300 seconds), then it's a good guess that your system's "block read" calls are taking around 0.004 seconds apiece.

It's a fun game to play, and it's more than just a magic trick: it is a testament to how well you understand the response time composition for the Create Invoice program. Until you catch the Create Invoice program in the act of misbehaving, you won't know for sure why it takes the time it does, but you do know that the program will be sensitive to fluctuations in "block read" call durations. And you know that if "block read" durations degrade by about a factor of ten (from 0.000 464 to 0.004 000), then Create Invoice response times will exceed five minutes.

So that's invoice creation from the perspective of its event durations. Now let's think about event counts: does Kevin's invoice creation feature make any unnecessary calls? Specifically, should creating an invoice really require 81,964 "block read" calls? That's enough to read the Bible 154 times.

A little investigating revealed that no, creating an invoice should never require nearly 82,000 reads. The program was in fact using an inefficient data access algorithm. Happily, it wasn't difficult to change the code to use a better algorithm that required fewer than 3,000 "block read" calls to produce a correct invoice.

The change significantly improved the invoice creation experience:

Subroutine	Duration	Count	Mean
block read	**0.864**	**2,603**	0.000 332
other	0.108	608	0.000 177
Total	**0.971**	3,211	0.000 302

With the change, creating an invoice takes only a second, which is over forty times faster than it used to be on its best days. The new profile is still sensitive to changes in "block read" response times (updating the spreadsheet will show you), but now if those response times were to degrade to 0.004 seconds, creating an invoice would take only about ten seconds. Yes, that's ten times worse than the new normal,[1] but it's still four times better than what was previously considered the best they could do.[2]

Eliminating unnecessary "block read" calls from each Create Invoice program execution helped Kevin's business in two ways:

The direct benefit

Eliminating almost 80,000 "block read" calls makes each Create Invoice execution go over eighty times faster,[3] which directly helps every customer who clicks that "Create Invoice" button.

The collateral benefit

Because the Create Invoice program runs a lot, especially near month-end, eliminating thousands of "block read" calls per execution eliminates millions of calls per hour. Eliminating so much load frees capacity on the SSD arrays that would have previously served these calls, which means less queueing and less likelihood of degraded "block read" response times. Faster call response times help not just invoicing but every program on the system that needs to execute "block read" calls.

The only "problem" is, we never did get a trace of the create invoice program behaving poorly. Because now it doesn't.

---

1 (10 seconds) / (0.971 seconds) ≈ 10.

2 (41.488 seconds) / (10 seconds) ≈ 4.

3 (85.452 seconds) / (0.971 seconds) ≈ 88.

41

Queueing Delay

Why would "block read" performance be fantastic early in the month, and then horrible later in the month? It's the same reason that riding Space Mountain® takes 10 minutes (yay!) when the park first opens, and then 90 minutes (ugh!) later that same morning. Even on healthy systems where everything is functioning properly, the more popular a resource gets, the longer you have to wait for it. It works that way for amusement parks, airport ticket counters, restaurants, highways, and—of course—computer components. It's unavoidable.

Here's how it happens. Let's go back to Kevin's story. Imagine that you are one of Kevin's customers, trying to grab your online invoice in the latter half of a month when the system is starting to get busy. As that Create Invoice program runs, it reaches the point in the code where it makes a "block read" call. On a lightly loaded system, that call would take one service time to complete.[1] But the SSD array can't start servicing your request right away, because it's already busy working on another request. In fact, there are *four* "block read" calls ahead of you in the queue: one call that's halfway done, and three others awaiting their turn.

So, your call gets in line. And waits.

Half a service time later, the call that was halfway done is finished. Three more service times later, the other three calls that were ahead of you are finished, and now it's your turn. One more service time later, for a total of 4.5 service times, your "block read" call is complete. Your response time for the call ends up being 0.002 088 seconds instead of the 0.000 464 that you'd have gotten earlier in the month.[2]

The difference between those two numbers is queueing delay.

---

1 On Kevin's system, an average service time was about 0.000 464 seconds.

2 $4.5 \times 0.000\ 464$ seconds = 0.002 088 seconds.

42

Queueing Theory

How great would *this* be: I tell you how busy I expect my system to get, and then you tell me how long my users will have to wait. Pretty nice, right? Because then you could help me decide how powerful a system I'd have to buy, and how much total work I could do. Well, there's a whole branch of mathematics called *queueing theory* that is devoted to helping you do just that.

Here is a plot of a queueing theory model called M/M/2,[1] which is a good model for predicting the behavior of Kevin's mirrored SSD array. It would also be a good model for, say, a two-lane highway, a public restroom with two stalls, or a bank with two tellers. The number "2" in "M/M/2" is the *service channel* count. A service channel is a resource that services requests; for example, an SSD, a lane, a stall, or a teller.

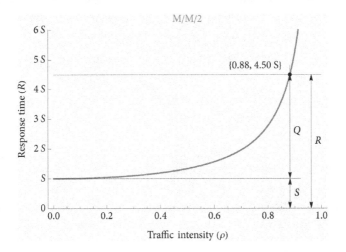

---

1 "M/M/c queue," Wikipedia, *https://oreil.ly/vmgPQ*.

This plot shows expected *response time* (R) as a function of *traffic intensity* (ρ), which is a measure from 0 to 1 of how busy the system is.[2] I've drawn the data from Kevin's SSD story in the plot: $R = Q + S = 4.5\ S$, where $Q = 3.5\ S$ is the expected queueing delay, and S is the expected service time. You could substitute the actual service time (0.000 464 seconds) for the symbol S, but it's easier to understand what's going on if you use S as the unit. That's why I've laid out the vertical axis in units of S.

Generally, the model reveals:

- Increasing the load on a system makes response times worse. The worsening happens gradually at lower loads and then rapidly at higher loads.

- As a system gets busier, it's not the service time (S) component that slows everyone down; it's the queueing delay (Q) component.

Specifically, for Kevin's example, you can observe:

- When your queue length was $Q = 3.5\ S$ (that is, when $R = 4.5\ S$), Kevin's SSD array must have been 88% busy. How do I know? I could have just eyeballed it and gotten pretty close, but I used a software tool called Mathematica to find what value of ρ makes R exactly equal to 4.5 S. That's one of the neat things about mathematical models: you can work them forwards or backwards, depending on what you're trying to accomplish.

- If you can keep Kevin's SSD from being more than about 50% busy, you can expect response times not to exceed about 1.5 service times.

- If you let Kevin's SSD become 90% busy, you should expect response times to be about five times worse than they'd be if your system were only about 20% busy.[3]

The picture that reveals all this information is just the plot of a formula you can find on the web.[4] Now that you've seen such a plot, you might be tempted to think that you should try to model every aspect of your system this way. I've learned to suppress that temptation. I will occasionally model a subsystem like I've done with Kevin's

---

2 The symbol for traffic intensity looks like a p, but ρ is the Greek letter rho.

3 This observation, by the way, should help you understand why eliminating wasteful calls helps everyone on the system collaterally.

4 "M/M/c," Wikipedia.

SSD, and it's always a thrill when the numbers match up. But most of the systems I work with are too complex to model this way.

For me, the greatest value of using models has been to fortify my understanding of how systems in general tend to behave. While I encourage you to experiment with queueing theory models if you're interested,[5] you'll be just fine if you dig no deeper than just reading what I've prepared for you here.

---

5 Certainly, you can code up one of the queueing theory models in Mathematica, or R, or Jupyter, or even Excel. But as with *any* model, don't wager too heavily on its predictions until you've proven through testing that those predictions are trustworthy.

43

The Hyperbola

It's important to know that queueing bends the response time curve into a hockey stick. Mathematically, it's a hyperbola. This shape is what defines the nature of queueing: response times will vary gently on systems with low traffic intensities, and they'll vary wildly on systems with high traffic intensities. Of course, big response time variances make interactive users especially miserable.

Your service channel count determines the bend in your hyperbola. M/M/1 systems have noticeable response time decay even at low traffic intensities. M/M/128 systems have virtually no decay throughout a broad range of traffic intensities, but then they decay violently at loads near $\rho = 1$.

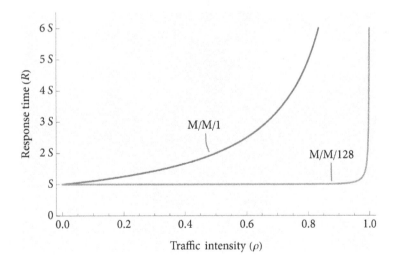

Expensive systems like M/M/128, whose R values stay flat longer as you add load, are what you'll use to handle ginormous high-concurrency workloads. But even the most scalable system on the planet will make you queue forever if you push its traffic intensity hard enough. That's why you need to stay a safe distance away from that skyward-pointing, righthand side of the curve, no matter what kind of system you're using.

What is a "safe distance"? You'll want to operate your system in the range of loads where tiny fluctuations in traffic intensity cause only tiny variances in response times. If there's so much load on your system that you can't do that, then you'll need to either eliminate load, reschedule load, or upgrade your system.

44

Traffic Intensity

The queueing theory plots I've shown illustrate the hyperbolic relationship between traffic intensity (ρ) and response time (R). Traffic intensity is a measure of how busy a resource is. Mathematically, traffic intensity is $\rho = \lambda S/c$—a function of three parameters: λ, S, and c.[1]

Arrival rate (λ)
> Traffic intensity varies directly with arrival rate, which is the pace at which requesters make service requests.

Service time (S)
> Traffic intensity varies directly with service time, which is the average response time of a request on an unloaded system.

Service channel count (c)
> Traffic intensity varies inversely with service channel count, which is the number of requests that can be processed in parallel. The service channel count is the c in the "M/M/c" plots I've been showing you.

You can manipulate traffic intensity by manipulating any of these three parameters. You reduce traffic intensity either by reducing event counts and event durations or by increasing the number of service channels.

---

1 Most textbooks define traffic intensity as $\rho = \lambda/(c\mu)$, where $\mu = 1/S$, but since $S = 1/\mu$, the formula I used here is equivalent, and it affords you and me both the luxury of not having to introduce another symbol μ (the service rate) for you to have to think about.

45

Utilization

Utilization (U) is just traffic intensity times the service channel count: $U = \rho c$. Since you're probably more familiar with utilization than traffic intensity, it might feel more comfortable to say it the other way around, that traffic intensity is just utilization with the service channel count divided out of it: $\rho = U/c$. Utilization and traffic intensity are exactly the same thing, just expressed in different units.

Since traffic intensity is always a number between 0 and 1, utilization is always a number between 0 and c. Utilization is often expressed as a percentage, using the "%" symbol to represent the quantity 0.01. For example, a system with four service channels will have traffic intensities and utilizations in the following ranges:

Metric	Range ($c = 4$)	
	Low	High
Traffic intensity	0	1
Utilization	0	4
Utilization as %	0%	400%

46

Hyperbolic Leverage

It's apparently human nature, at least among my English-speaking friends, to imagine the response time hyperbola as something that one would normally only climb, moving from left to right as one adds load to a system. Of course, as you move left to right, you accumulate pain at—literally—a *hyperbolic* pace.

But left to right is not the only option. As you know, you can also *reduce* a system's traffic intensity, which is a ride from right to left. And that's not a hockey stick; that's a ski slope!

Take a moment to consider what riding down that ski slope represents. If you're on a system with high traffic intensity, like Kevin's system at month-end, then imagine what will happen if you could reduce the traffic intensity by even just a little bit. Of course, as you move from right to left, you eliminate pain at—literally—a hyperbolic pace!

By understanding that hyperbola—that hockey stick—you should be able to more clearly imagine the tremendous leverage we accessed when we changed that data access algorithm in Kevin's Create Invoice program, to eliminate millions of unnecessary "block read" calls (request arrivals) per hour.

47

Coherency Delay

Queueing degrades response times as your traffic intensity increases. A second type of delay is called *coherency delay*. Coherency delay is the duration required to make data consistent, or *cache coherent*, by virtue of point-to-point exchange of data between distributed resources.[1]

Imagine a distributed system that runs on two separate computers (nodes). Each node has its own master cache. But when an application on node A requests a page from its cache, it has to execute extra instructions to check whether there's a newer copy of the same page in the node B cache. If there is, then node A will need to fetch a copy of that page from node B. The extra instructions required to maintain cache coherency lengthen the service time of the page access.

Coherency delays can be particularly corrosive. Whereas queueing delays degrade only the Q component of $R = Q + S$, coherency delays degrade the S component, which creates *two* problems. Obviously making S bigger will make $R = anything + S$ the same amount bigger. But, worse than that, increasing S increases traffic intensity, which increases Q as well. Coherency delays thus affect response times at high loads by more than just the service time increase.

---

1 Neil Gunther, "How to Quantify Scalability: The Universal Scalability Law (USL)." *https://oreil.ly/yhO-J*, 2020.

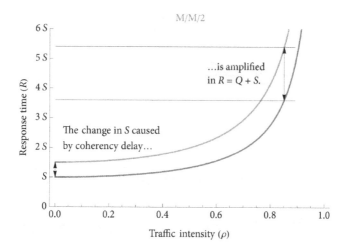

On the bright side, if you have a lot of coherency delay, then eliminating even just a little bit of it may significantly improve the performance of your system. The hyperbola punishes you as loads increase, but it rewards you bountifully for reducing load when you can.

48

Delays and Throughput

Queueing and coherency delays degrade response times. Of course, they degrade throughput as well. Here's the throughput effect of queueing delay:[1]

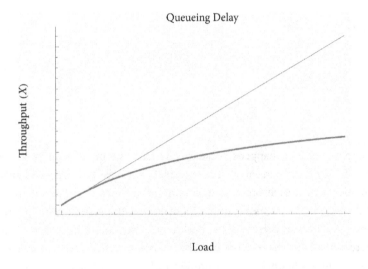

The curve that we'd all love to be on is that straight line, where every new unit of concurrent workload you add increases throughput by as much as the previous unit you added. But the effect of queueing is to diminish the marginal utility of adding load.

---

1 Gunther, "The Universal Scalability Law (USL)."

Adding coherency delay degrades throughput even more. Notice how, in the following plot, the throughput curve actually bends *downward* as loads increase past the point labeled "peak throughput." This downward bend creates stories like, "We added an order entry clerk, and now our system processes fewer orders per minute than before."

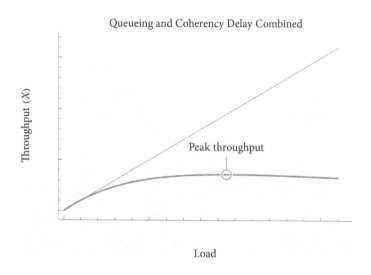

This retrograde behavior happens because coherency is a manifestation of the ramp problem (which I'll explain later). Imagine that you have ten processes that must all communicate with each other to maintain cache coherency. Then there are 9 + 8 + 7 + ... + 1 = 45 communication channels that the system must maintain. If the number of processes increases just by 1, to 11, then the communication channel count increases by 10, to 55. Doubling the process count from 10 to 20 increases the communication channel count from 55 to 210. The number of communication channels varies in proportion to the square of the process count.

It's really ugly. It's why you need to design as much coherency delay *out* of your system as you can.

PART VII

Waste

49

Debra

My friend Debra is a consultant. In 2005, she visited a large publishing company for a routine checkup that she schedules for six months after helping a client go live with a new enterprise resource planning (ERP) system. Things were in pretty good shape, so it was a pretty easy engagement. The company's biggest issue had been some slow queries in the General Ledger. She fixed those by creating a new index.

When she asked whether there was anything else she could do to help, the manager she'd been working with said no, but the clerk who sat behind him said, "*I* have a problem." The manager seemed embarrassed, but Debra pressed the clerk, and he continued, "Every day I throw away reams of paper from our invoice listing."

Debra asked to look at the job request in the application. The job request ran a program to print an invoice list every day at a scheduled time. On the schedule screen, she found a checkbox labeled "Increment date on each run." Checked, the program would list only the invoices entered since the last time the program ran. Unchecked, the program would list all the invoices that had ever been created on the system. The checkbox was, oops, unchecked.

So, every day, the company had been listing every invoice that had ever been created since day one of the project. On day two, when the program listed twice as many invoices as it had on day one, it wouldn't have been a big enough problem to notice. But a couple months in, the reports would have been 50+ times longer than on day one. By the six-month mark, the waste of paper would have been staggering.

The solution? Debra checked the box ☑. From then on, the invoice listing program listed only the invoices created since its prior execution. That's it. A simple but complete solution to a problem that had been getting worse every day.

Debra did two important things that will work for you, too:

She looked at the right it
>   She could have called it a day when the manager acted like he didn't want to talk about the clerk's problem, but she pressed the clerk about the issue and ended up relieving an important symptom.

She filtered early
>   She filtered unwanted invoice listings before they were even requested, instead of filtering them at the trash can after printing.

50

The Ramp

In Debra's story, the clerk said that he was throwing away *reams* of paper every day. A ream is a pack of 500 sheets. Surely he was exaggerating, right?

Well, let's figure it out. Debra told me that the company was creating about 1,000 new invoices per weekday and that they could list 66 invoices per page on the invoice report. That means there were about 16 new pages' worth of invoices being created every day. With the "Increment date on each run" box unchecked, the invoice listing report had been growing about 16 sheets thicker every day:

Day (n)	Sheets printed $(16\,n)$
1	16
2	32
3	48
...	...
128	2,048
129	2,064
130	2,080

On the day before Debra's six-month checkup visit (about 130 weekdays after going live), the clerk would have thrown away over 2,000 sheets of paper. That's more than four full 500-sheet reams discarded in just one day. The clerk was *not* exaggerating.

This performance antipattern, where experiences gradually worsen over time, is called the *ramp*.[1]

---

[1] Connie Smith and Lloyd Williams, "New Software Performance AntiPatterns: More Ways to Shoot Yourself in the Foot," 2002, *https://oreil.ly/IQTca*.

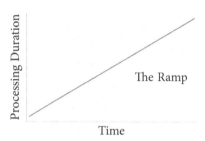

As annoying as the ramp is, the gradual processing duration creep isn't the worst of it. Over time, the cumulative resource consumption becomes the much bigger issue:

	Sheets used	
Day one day		to-date
(n)	($16\,n$)	($16\,n(n + 1)/2$)
1	16	16
2	32	48
3	48	96
...	...	...
130	2,080	136,240

It adds up fast. After six months of creating 16 pages' worth of new invoices per day, they'd have used 136,240 sheets of paper for invoice listings. That's 273 reams! And all but 2,080 of these sheets would be duplicated waste.

A little math can help you understand the gravity of the problem. The sum of the numbers 1 through n is given by the formula $n(n + 1)/2$. For example, $1 + 2 + 3 + \ldots + 10 = 10\,(10 + 1)/2 = 55$. So a program that prints 16 pages per day will have printed $16\,n(n + 1)/2$ pages after the nth execution of the invoice listing (after the nth day post–go-live). The number of *wasted* pages is that quantity minus $16\,n$, which simplifies to $16\,(n^2 - n)/2$. And that's the big problem: the waste is proportional to the *square* of your execution count.

Squaring is a monstrous magnifier. When cost varies as the square of something, it slaughters your efficiency. When your *something* doubles, your cost quadruples. When your *something* increases by 10×, your cost increases by 100×. When your *something* increases 100-fold, cost increases 10,000-fold.

You can't fight a square with a line. For example, printing double-sided instead of single-sided won't solve this problem. Sure, you'll cut your waste in half, but over time, the square will still eat you up. Debra's client was destined to become the Dunder Mifflin *Customer of the Century*, had they not solved this problem. By the end of just one year (260 workdays), they would have burned through 542,880 sheets of paper. That's 1,086 reams. But with the checkbox checked, they would have needed only 4,160 sheets, which is less than nine reams for the whole year.

Difference between 542,880 sheets and merely 4,160 (shown in 10-ream cases)

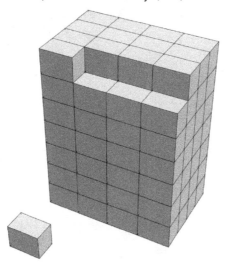

The ramp at Debra's client is a story about wasted paper, but it's not just a paper problem. There's also the CPU, memory, disk, and network capacity that is consumed by printing all those unwanted pages. It affects everyone, not just the clerks who look after invoices. The waste adds load to the system, which causes competition for scarce resources, which slows everybody down.

Some problems you can just live with. The ramp is not one of them. The gradual creep may seem innocuous, but the square in the cumulative resource consumption will eventually take you down. You've *got* to get rid of your ramps.

Martha

Once in 1995, I had a week where I'd be visiting two clients. On Monday, I'd fly from my home near Dallas to Detroit and spend the morning downtown. Then I'd fly to Columbia, South Carolina to spend a few days. My first day would be tight. I wouldn't have time in Detroit to grab lunch, and I knew the regional airline that would get me to Columbia wouldn't serve food. When I landed, there'd be a car waiting to take me to the meeting, where a group of angry men and women would be waiting for me.

My wife suggested that I take a sandwich. I could eat it in the car after my meeting, between downtown Detroit and the airport. She even asked what I wanted and made it for me: ham, cheese, mayonnaise, white bread, a Ziploc bag, and a napkin.

When I arrived in Detroit, I rented a car and drove downtown. In my client's parking garage, I had to decide what to do with the sandwich. My choices were to put it into my briefcase, where it would get all smashed, or leave it in the car. It was a cool morning. Detroit was "way up north" compared to my home in Dallas, and my car would be in the shade the whole time. I'd be done before noon, so—I figured—it would probably still be cool when I got back to the car. So, I left the sandwich on the front seat.

When I left my meeting, it was surprisingly hot out, around 90°F. Inside the car it must have been at least 120°F. When I pulled the door handle, the door popped open on a wave of hot, compressed air that had been trapped inside the car. The Ziploc bag was a puffy little square balloon. Not good.

So I started my drive to the airport. There I was, a grown man in a suit and tie, with a flight to catch, and I was still actually considering eating that sandwich. If I eat it, then I might get sick. But I might not. If I don't eat it, then of course I'd be hungry, and I'd waste the sandwich. That my wife had made for me.

Somehow I was able to justify holding onto the original plan. Maybe it had been so hot in the car that the sandwich was just fine…the same as if it had been in an oven all morning. Or under a heat lamp. I ate the whole sandwich in the car on the way to the airport.

The flight from Detroit to Columbia was a twin-turboprop aircraft, probably an ATR 42 or something like it. It was a smooth ride until the turbulence hit on our final descent. It took me a minute to realize that the turbulence wasn't coming from the airplane, it was coming from my abdomen. Not good.

I arrived at my customer site functional but just barely. There were thirty people waiting for me in a tiered auditorium. The meeting would begin with people taking turns on the stage at the front of the room explaining their anger and frustration. Before too long, I would need to take the stage myself, to calm everybody down and convince them that I had a process they could trust.

When I arrived, it was hard to imagine being able to do that. It felt like my guts had all melted. I was spending more time in the restroom than in the meeting. I sat in the top row of the auditorium, right by the door, so I wouldn't disrupt the meeting during the many departures and arrivals to and from the men's room. One of my teammates named Tom sat there on the top row with me and took good notes during all my absences.

At this point in the story, I'm sorry, but it will be necessary for me to explain in graphic detail about what was happening in that restroom.

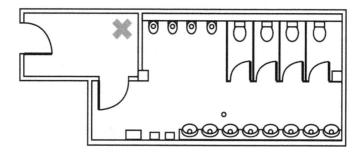

This is the floor plan of a restroom that's similar to the one I was visiting. The door at the top left was the entry from the hallway. The second door got you into the restroom itself. The two-door design prevents people in the hallway from seeing people in the restroom when the entry door is open. The space between the two doors ends up being the perfect spot to temporarily store used printer paper that was destined for recycling (✖ marks the spot in my drawing).

The first time I went to the restroom, I wasn't in the mood to notice much, but I did see a stack of that green-bar fanfold paper that came all the way up to my belt level. It was *so much* paper, probably ten thousand pages. The next time I visited, about ten minutes later, the stack was shorter, only up to my knees. As I kept visiting the restroom every few minutes, the stack height was always different from before—sometimes bigger, sometimes smaller. My fifth visit or so, I held the door for a man wearing coveralls who was there with a hand truck to take away the now–chest-high stack of paper for recycling.

I asked him, "Hey, do you mind if I take a little bit of that paper before you haul it off?"

He told me, "I don't mind at all. All the confidential stuff goes into a locked bin at another location. Take all you want."

So I tapped the top edge of the stack, and a half-inch chunk rotated off. I took that chunk with me, curious, and hoping to divert my attention while my insides tried to finish expressing their hostility at my decision not to "waste" that sandwich. The report I took was labeled "General Ledger Trial Balance Report." I didn't have much of an idea what it was beyond its name.

Eventually, back in the auditorium, it was my turn to take the stage. By then, I was good to go. Tom had found me a box of Imodium A-D®.[1]

So I drew on the whiteboard and explained about the behavior of queueing and how the process we'd use would provide relief for the symptoms they'd been enduring. One important element of that process would be to eliminate unnecessary load, which would be especially vital here, since their system was operating too close to its max capacity. This kind of talk got us through the tricky listen–calm–convince parts of the project.

The next day, I visited the stack during a routine men's room visit and confirmed that nearly the whole thing was these trial balance reports. What *were* these things? And why were there so many of them? Were they all necessary? Obviously, computing enough data to fill this much paper was probably putting a lot of load on the system.

---

1 If you, dear reader, are either Tom, or you worked for Johnson & Johnson in the mid-1990s, thank you for your service.

The person who would know all the answers was a colleague named Martha. Martha (her real name) was the accounting expert in charge of the functional aspects of the client's recently installed Oracle Financial and Manufacturing application software. Her desk was nearby, so I walked over to see her.

I asked her up front to please forgive my indelicacy, but I had a story about the men's restroom that I needed to tell her. I had estimated—correctly, as it turned out—that Martha might not have been aware of the various goings-on with the big paper stack in there. I told her that there were thousands of pages being hauled off for recycling every hour or so, and it was pretty much all trial balance reports.

She smiled and thanked me for letting her know. This was indeed important information. She would disable that report so that nobody would be able to run it again. I didn't expect *that*. Just turn it off?!

"You see," she explained, "in double-entry accounting, every transaction gets a debit entry and a matching credit entry. If at the end of the day, the sums of the debits don't match the sums of the credits, then an accountant has to find and fix the error that must have occurred. This report tells them which accounts they need to investigate, and it gives the detail they need to diagnose the problem."

I asked the obvious question. It seemed like this checking–finding–fixing process she described would be important.

"Right," she told me. "We *do* need that feature, but we *don't* need the report. What they're *accustomed* to doing is, they'll run this huge report—you've seen how thick they are—and then they'll look at the last page. If it's all zeros, they throw the whole report on the recycle pile without even looking at the other pages. If the last page is not all zeros, then they start looking through the report to find where the error came from.

"But they don't need to do it that way anymore. There's a screen in the new application that shows the accountant only those accounts where the debits and credits don't match up, and then she can drill in from there. It's all online now. There's no need to run that report again. Ever."

Turning off that report eliminated something like 10% of the total CPU work done by the system. Disabling that report was a big, easy win for performance, systemwide, because it slid them leftward down their CPU hyperbola.

So, keep your eyes open. Stay curious. Opportunities can pop up literally anywhere. I might never have seen this one, had it not been for that lucky sandwich I ate in Detroit.

52

Efficiency

Efficiency is getting the output you want for the least possible investment of input. It is an inverse measure of waste. Efficiency is how you flourish on a budget. To a performance analyst, eliminating waste—to get more from less—should feel like a genetic imperative.

An *efficient program* is one that produces correct and useful output with the least possible amount of work. The trial balance report that Martha disabled was inefficient by its mere existence: it didn't matter how efficient its code was or wasn't, the trial balance reports were wasteful because they weren't useful. Kevin's invoicing program, though both correct and useful, was inefficient due to a data access algorithm that did more work than necessary.

An *efficient system* is a system that executes only programs that are necessary and efficient. Do you notice how it always comes back to the thing the user experiences—the thing you're supposed to be *looking at*? It's no coincidence. Performance matters where the user is. Thus, it's important to know how to measure the efficiency of your programs. With profiles, it's easy. A program is efficient if and only if:

- It produces correct and useful output; and
- It executes no unnecessary events (calls, instructions, etc.).

Just to be clear, when I say "a program" (or "it"), I mean all the code your program executes or causes to be executed, including its own code and all of the subroutines it executes, including both user library calls and system library calls. All the way down to the metal. So when, for example, an application program runs slowly because a database parameter causes more cache visits than you really needed, then I'm saying that the program is making unnecessary calls.

53

Fix It, or Feed It?

So, do you fix an inefficiency? Or do you feed it?

A lot of people feed inefficiencies. I can't count the number of places I've been where the attempted solution before my visit had been some kind of a hardware upgrade. But there are lots of situations where adding hardware just won't help. The Payroll story is a good example. The forty-nine grievances story contains several others.

In many situations, of course, a hardware upgrade *can* help. Take Kevin's story, for example. It's easy to imagine the secondary storage upgrade that I'm sure his team had bought before I met him. Upgrading from conventional HDDs to SSDs probably reduced average "block read" durations from maybe 0.002 seconds to the 0.000 464 seconds that I saw. Such an upgrade would have resulted in invoice creations taking 40 seconds instead of something closer to 200. A victory worth celebrating.

However, they could have reduced invoice response times from 200 seconds to about 5 seconds, without moving to SSD, if they had fixed the program's data access algorithm. Of course, the faster hardware is nice to have, but maybe 5-second invoices, with no spooky stuff at month-end, would have satisfied the business without having to make a hardware investment at all. After that, if they had needed invoicing to run even faster, they could have made a calculated decision to buy those SSD arrays, to reduce invoice response times to less than a second.

The *fix-or-feed* decision comes down to trust. Maybe you don't trust the *fix* option because you've hired people before who claimed that they could make your system faster but didn't. And buying hardware: well, that's safe, right? It's at least an asset with objective value, whether it does everything you expect or not. …But, of course, if you've lived through a hardware upgrade that didn't work out like you wanted, then maybe you don't particularly trust the *feed* option, either.

It seems like an intractable problem, but the solution is harmonious with everything else I've written in this book: if you're intimate with your highest-priority programs' profiles, then you can make well-informed decisions about whether you should *fix* (that is, reduce some event counts) or *feed* (reduce some event durations). You'll want to do some combination of *fix* and *feed* that will produce the greatest net benefit for the investment you're willing to risk.

The need for optimization skills doesn't diminish as technology makes the *feed* option easier, by the way. For example, the new elastic cloud computing services now on the market make feeding a system easier than it's ever been: adding capacity to your system becomes frictionless. But the economics of such systems incentivize their users to trim their workload as much as they can, because every cycle they use, they pay for.

54

Yeti

In conference presentations, sometimes I ask, "How many of you have ever experienced a hardware upgrade where the system wasn't as much faster after the upgrade as you had hoped?" Usually about 90% of my audience members raise their hand. Then I ask, "OK, how many of you have ever experienced a hardware upgrade where the system became *objectively slower* after the upgrade?" Usually only about 5% of people in the room raise their hand, and those hand-raises are usually timid. Even the people who've seen it aren't sure whether they believe it. It's the natural self-doubt inspired by a Yeti sighting.

But it's true; it happens. Upgrades to faster hardware can make important programs go slower. And I can explain why. I can even tell you when to expect it to happen. There's nothing supernatural about it.

When Jeff and I visited our Payroll client in Dallas, I had never actually seen evidence for an upgrade making an application slower. But that day we saw an irrefutable case of an upgrade making a high-priority program objectively slower. And we had the data. We had a big ol' Yeti in a net.

Remember, this was a client whose PYUGEN process was running so slowly that they couldn't print paychecks on time. After suffering for months, they finally bit the bullet and upgraded their CPUs, hoping it would fix PYUGEN. But, to their horror, PYUGEN was objectively slower after the upgrade.

When we arrived, we traced a PYUGEN execution for half an hour, resulting in this profile:

Subroutine	Duration		Count	Mean
	seconds	%		
SQL*Net message from client	984.010	50.3%	95,161	0.010 340
SQL*Net more data from client	418.820	21.4%	3,345	0.125 208
db file sequential read	279.340	14.3%	45,084	0.006 196
CPU service, EXEC calls	136.880	7.0%	67,888	0.002 016
CPU service, PARSE calls	74.490	3.8%	10,098	0.007 377
CPU service, FETCH calls	37.320	1.9%	57,217	0.000 652
latch free	23.690	1.2%	34,695	0.000 683
8 other subroutines	2.920	0.1%	111,829	0.000 026
Total (15)	1,957.470	100.0%	425,317	0.004 602

Here's how a perfectly good CPU upgrade made PYUGEN slower:

- PYUGEN had never used much CPU to begin with. It used about 249 seconds on the faster 1 GHz CPUs,[1] so it probably used about 364 seconds on the slower 700 MHz CPUs.[2] The upgrade probably saved PYUGEN about 115 seconds of CPU time.[3]

- The CPU upgrade did help some heavy CPU-consuming programs on the system spend less time using CPU, but nobody cared, because those programs were unimportant in the shadow of their Payroll problem.

- After the upgrade, each heavy CPU-consuming program made the same number of network I/O calls as it had made before the upgrade. But, with faster CPUs now, each program ran more quickly. This increased the network's arrival rate, which increased its traffic intensity.

- The increased traffic intensity of the network, whose average service time was already inflated by the configuration mistake, increased network queueing delays, moving users to the right along the network's response time hyperbola.

---

1 (136.880 + 74.490 + 37.320) seconds ≈ 249 seconds.

2 (1024 MHz / 700 MHz) × 248.690 seconds ≈ 364 seconds.

3 (364 – 249) seconds ≈ 115 seconds.

- PYUGEN ended up slower than before the CPU upgrade because the upgrade impaired PYUGEN's network performance by more than the 115 seconds of CPU time that it saved.

The failure of the upgrade to fix the PYUGEN problem was a great shock to our client, but it didn't need to be. Had they profiled PYUGEN before the upgrade, they'd have known beyond a shadow of a doubt that upgrading CPUs, no matter how fast the new ones would be, could never cut PYUGEN's time in half. It was an inevitable consequence of Amdahl's law: PYUGEN had never used enough CPU for a CPU upgrade to help that much.

So, here's the lesson. Catching a Yeti is a lot of fun—as long as it's somebody *else's* Yeti. To prevent a Yeti from ruining *your* day, do these two things:

- Understand the *priorities* of the programs your business uses.
- Understand the *profiles* of your high-priority programs.

55

Fast vs. Efficient

Fast and *efficient* are different. An inefficient program can be fast, and an efficient program can be slow. Neither implies the other. For example, Kevin's team considered their invoice program "fast" when it ran in 40 seconds, even though it was grossly inefficient (executing about 80,000 more "block read" calls per execution than it should have). On the other hand, even a program with perfect efficiency will run slowly on a system that is too busy.

Efficient is an objective measure of waste; it's all about event counts. But *fast* is different. Of course, an execution's speed is objectively measurable, either as a response time or a throughput. But whether that speed is considered *fast* or *slow* depends upon what you *expect* about it. Whether an execution is *fast* or *slow* is subjective. It's an agreement.

One of Kevin's team members said in a call one day, "If my cell phone service provider's website made me wait 40 seconds for my invoice, I'd probably switch to another provider." The team accepted their own 40-second response times because they grudgingly assumed there was no way to make invoicing go faster. But when they improved the code to take less than a second instead of 40+, it reset the team's tolerances. With the new remedied code, 40 seconds isn't fast anymore. What was fast yesterday is unacceptable today.

56

Scalability

Scalability is a mathematical property with a precise definition. It is the rate of change of speed with respect to a specified parameter. Here is an example. The following plot shows the speed (measured as response time) of four data access algorithms with respect to the number of rows in a table. The curves are all labeled in what mathematicians call "big O" notation,[1] which describes the shape of the curve. The interesting question is: which of the four algorithms is best?

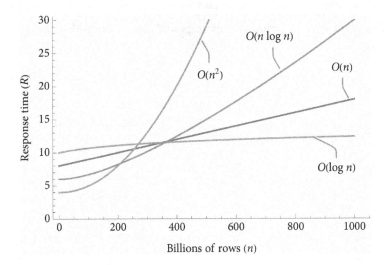

The answer is: it depends upon the row count of your table. If it has fewer than 200 billion rows, then the $O(n^2)$ algorithm will give better response time than any of the other algorithms. Between 200 billion and 400 billion rows, the $O(n \log n)$ algorithm

---

1 $O(n^2)$, for example, is pronounced "big-oh of *n* squared."

is best. If it has more than 400 billion rows, then the $O(\log n)$ algorithm is going to give you the best response time.

The R value on a curve for a given n value is the *speed* of an algorithm at a given data set size. The shape of its curve is the algorithm's *scalability*. While the particular $O(n^2)$ algorithm in this plot does give better performance for smaller tables, the $O(\log n)$ algorithm is more scalable with respect to table size because it gives better performance as your table size grows toward infinity.

You can measure scalability with respect to any parameter that influences performance. For example:

- How an algorithm's response time scales with respect to input data volume (as in the example I've plotted)
- How a program's response time scales with respect to concurrent user count
- How a program's throughput scales with respect to concurrent user count
- How a program's throughput or response time scales with respect to CPU core count

PART VIII

Problem Solving

Four Simple Questions

Profiles are familiar from everyday life. Here's one you may recognize:

```
Qty  Item              Price   Amount
  4  Heineken           4.50    18.00
  2  Soft Drink         2.09     4.18
  1  Baja Chicken      12.95    12.95
  1  Brisket Nachos    13.45    13.45
  2  Finger Basket      8.95    17.90
              Subtotal           66.48
                   Tax            1.83
              Total              68.31
```

Of course, that's a restaurant receipt. But it's a *profile* for an expenditure. Customers appreciate this format because it makes it easy to see how much their meal cost and why. The format makes it easy to see what your bill would have been if you'd ordered just one round of beers instead of two.

The same format also makes it easy to answer questions about why it takes 40 minutes to get an order confirmation number, or what will happen to PYUGEN if you can reduce your average network round-trip duration by a factor of 55.

The power of the profile—this receipt for a user's response time—is that it answers four simple questions that give you the fastest path for relieving your business's important symptoms. Those four simple questions are:

1. *How long?*

How long did the execution take? The answer is the bottom line of a profile. If your symptom is a throughput problem, then your inquiry will begin with a *how-many* question but still evolve to a *how-long* question for your individual task executions.

2. *Why?*

Why did the execution consume the time that it did? The event counts and durations (quantities and prices) in your profile identify the causes for the symptom you're diagnosing.

3. *What if?*

Once you know how long an execution took and why, you can begin considering cures for the causes you see. The profile lets you use simple arithmetic to predict how much time a potential cure will save.

4. *What else?*

After you've implemented a cure, an *after* profile helps you prove whether you've actually relieved the symptom you care about. Then, you'll loop back to the *how-long* question for more relief of the same symptom, or for the next symptom on your prioritized list.

These four questions are simple because they reject all the junk that doesn't matter. They are focused on exactly what *you* should be focused on. Answering them head-on is the most direct path you can take to improving performance.

These questions are so obvious that they're natural even for children to ask. But there's a problem: unless you know how to trace and profile a program execution, they're nearly impossible to answer. Without tracing and profiling, they become the four *awkward* questions that you hope nobody asks.

What I see in the field is that when people have a question they can't answer, they tend to settle for asking a different question that they *can* answer. This substitute question is usually a weaker version of the original (though it might look more sophisticated). Reframing a question might seem innocent, but it can be treacherous. For example, contrast the relative merits of the following questions and their weaker surrogates:

Your real question:	Its weaker surrogate:
"How long does it take Payroll to process 890 assignments?"	"How long do Payroll's individual SQL statements run?"
"Why does Payroll take 33 minutes to process 890 assignments?"	"What is the most-used resource on the system while Payroll is running?"
"Should we focus on reducing network round-trip time, which accounts for 70% of response time? Or reducing CPU consumption, which accounts for 10%?"	"What do you think would happen if we were to spend $20,000 on a CPU upgrade?"
"Now that we've cut the response time in half, are there events on the new profile that deserve further investigation?"	"The CPU upgrade didn't help; what else could we try?"

There's no comparison. When you've answered the four simple questions, you know exactly what's going on. When you've answered only the surrogates? The Payroll tragedy illustrates where that can lead you.

58

Reaching the End of Your Data

The *how-long–why* loop is a tidy way to think about performance. Every response time problem, at its highest level of analysis, is a *how-long* problem. How long did PYUGEN take in the Payroll story? 1,957 seconds. Likewise, every price problem, at its highest level of analysis, is a *how-much* problem. How much did your bag of groceries cost? $55.48. In both worlds, the next question you'll ask is *why*.

Answering the *why* question requires an analytical plunge, a drill-down that you can accomplish only if you have more detailed data to drill into. If you know that PYUGEN took 1,957 seconds only because you timed it with a stopwatch, then you're not going to be able to answer the *why* question until you trace. Likewise, if all you see is the $55.48 line item on your credit card statement, you won't be able to answer *why* until you find your receipt.

Every *how-long* question stimulates its own *why*. The process is recursive, because each new *why* inspires a new, more detailed *how-long* (or *how-much*) question that can inspire a new *why* question, like this:

	The users are upset.	*Mom's upset.*
Why?	Because Payroll is taking too long	Because the tomatoes cost too much
How long/ much?	1,957 seconds	$15.48
Why?	Because 984 sec (50%) is network I/O calls	Because $15.48 (100%) is tomatoes (after returning the chocolate bars)
How long/ much?	95,161 calls costing 10 msec per call	1.2 lb of tomatoes costing $12.90/lb
Why?	That detail is not available in the trace	That detail is not available on the receipt

Answering a *why* question advances your understanding a step beyond the *how-long* that stimulated it. But the drill-downs last only as long as you have further detail to drill into. Eventually, your detail runs out. The PYUGEN profile revealed that our network read calls averaged 10 msec apiece, but it didn't explain *why* they lasted that long, or even whether that duration was reasonable.

It's the same with the tomatoes. The receipt revealed that the store charged you $12.90 per pound, but it didn't explain why. So unless you'd bought tomatoes recently, you might not even know whether $12.90 was reasonable. In both cases, you've reached the end of your data, and to make progress, you'll have to learn something beyond what the data you've collected can tell you.

The way forward in the tomato story is to visit the customer service desk. Maybe there's a transportation strike and tomatoes really do cost that much now. Maybe there's a nationwide tomato blight. Maybe it's inflation. You could guess for months. But there's no need to guess; just ask. The answer? The price was a data-entry error. Someone had typed $12.9 instead of $1.29.

But with PYUGEN, whom do you ask? The product documentation is usually a good place to begin. In our case, Jeff was able to propose a high-value cure so quickly because he already knew how SQL*Net worked—he knew it had a beneficial feature that our customer wasn't using. A quick experiment proved that he was correct.

With good trace data, you'll usually find your cure before your detail runs out. But even if you don't, you won't be empty-handed. You'll at least know how much time is being consumed, and you'll know exactly how important that number is to your overall response time. With this information, you'll never need to wonder whether your attention is focused on the right question for making progress. Progress will be just a matter of learning more about what's going on. That could mean reading, asking questions, gathering more data, or creating an experiment.

59

Your C-Level Feedback Loop

Knowing *how-long* is the key to answering two questions that will define the primary interface between your project team and the people who are counting on you to succeed.[1] The questions your C-level executives are going to need you to answer are:

1. If we do *x*, will it relieve our symptom? How much?
2. We did *x*. Did it relieve our symptom? How much?

These are really the same question, just asked at different points on a timeline. An executive will ask the first question prior to an investment, and the second one after the investment. Together, they form a feedback loop: the first question uses incomplete information to stimulate an action, and the second question uses more-complete information to evaluate how successful that action was (and by implication, how successful *you* were).

The best way to answer the *how-long* question is by tracing. You could also answer it with a stopwatch (or a sundial if the problem is bad enough), but a trace is better, because it prepares you to answer the *why*, *what-if*, and *what-else* questions that are coming next.

---

1 Or, depending on your circumstance, *how-many* or *how-much*.

60

Collateral Damage

One early afternoon in a yellow house a few miles outside of Copenhagen, several friends and I were visiting together from all over the world for a conference. It was January, which means that outside it was dark and raining and about a thousandth of a degree above freezing. Inside, though, was a totally different story. I felt unbearably hot. As I made my way over to the exterior door to get some fresh air, it occurred to me that perhaps fanning the door a time or two might make the room more comfortable. However, before doing so, my manners kicked in, and I asked if anybody would mind if I fanned in some cold air.

One of my friends from Holland looked up from his laptop and said bluntly (as Dutch friends will do), "Why don't you just take off your fokking sweater?" At this point I realized that indeed I was still wearing a heavy sweater, made from layers of GoreTex®, Thinsulate™, and Icelandic lambswool, with a zippered collar that went up to my ears. It was equipment exceptionally well suited for the outdoor Danish climate, where, at the time, I happened not to be. When I took it off, I was comfortable and happy, and of course the solution that my friend had so delicately suggested hadn't messed up the interior weather for anyone else in the room.

It's the same for all kinds of systems: improving one experience can accidentally degrade another. Here are some other examples:

- Using the car to make your errand faster causes your spouse to be late for a meeting.
- Upgrading CPUs in the Payroll story made some programs faster, but it made PYUGEN slower. The same thing would have happened if the company had eliminated wasted CPU consumption from the low-priority programs running at the same time as PYUGEN.

- Creating database indexes to make your TPS report go faster can slow down the big batch insert process that was already struggling.

So, what should you do?

- Keep the scope of your cure proportional to the scope of your symptom.
- Don't make global parameter changes when local ones will suffice.
- Understand the priorities of the programs on your system. Before you upgrade your system, make sure that your highest priority programs are actually starved for the resources you're upgrading.
- Consider the global scenario. When you change your system for one program, consider the impact of those changes upon other programs. Good integration tests should be able to alert you to occurrences of collateral damage before you inflict them upon a production system.

61

Too Much of a
Good Thing

In Oracle courses, I teach people about an application parameter whose setting can have a profound influence over response times.[1] I show students that, for the particular application we're studying, changing the value of this parameter from 1 to 2 will cut response time in half. Setting it to 4 cuts response time in half again. Setting it to 8, 16, 32, and 64 cuts it in half again four more times.

At this point, I say cheerfully, "Just think how fast this application would perform if we could set the parameter's value to a million-trillion." I pause for a few seconds to let that question sink in. Then I show them the punch line: when you try to use 16,384, you get an out-of-memory error. A response time of infinity.

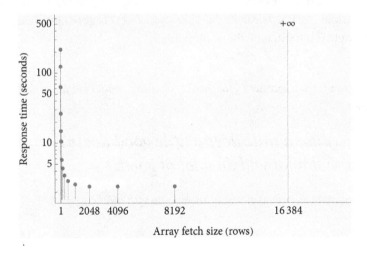

1 It's the application's array fetch size, if you're curious.

This is the "bathtub-shaped curve" that engineers talk about. The left wall of the tub shows the happy goodness of response times getting better and better. Then there's a flat spot at the bottom, where response times don't improve perceptibly, as you continue doubling the parameter. And, inevitably, there's a right wall, which forms the tub shape, where response time becomes—in this case—infinitely bad. The lesson: it's vital to give this parameter a good value, but 16,384 is too much of a good thing.

To help lock that idea into my students' minds, I like to tell the story of how I learned the "too much of a good thing" lesson as a kid.

Throughout my life, I've had these awful, soul-crushing headaches. Lately I've not had so many, thankfully. I can remember having them as a kid: one minute, I'd be outside playing; the next minute, I'd be wiped out. I'd make my way back to the house from whatever I'd been doing, and my Mom would give me two tablets from a bottle of Anacin© with a glass of water. I would lie down and cover my eyes with a cold, wet washcloth. About 30 minutes later, I would feel fine again, and I would carry on living.

One time when I was around ten years old, I told my Mom how fortunate I felt about having these pills available that could relieve this pain, which, at that point in my life was the worst I had ever experienced. My Mom, recognizing the teachable moment opportunity, said, "If just two pills can make you feel this good, just imagine how good you would feel if you took the whole bottle!"

What?!

I thought about it for a second. "That would, uh…that would *kill* me, right?" "Right," she told me:

Just because a little does a little good doesn't mean that a lot will do a lot of good.

Both of my parents enjoyed that whole Socratic thing. I did, too.

62

Doug

Doug was a director at a Kansas City company with exceptionally high order volumes. One of my team's assignments in 1994 was to draft Doug a plan for a high-availability architecture that would offer "five nines" of uptime. Getting to five nines means no more than about 5 minutes of downtime per year.

Nines	Uptime	Downtime per year
1	0.9	36d 12h
2	0.99	3d 15h 36m
3	0.999	8h 45m 36s
4	0.999 9	52m 33.6s
5	0.999 99	5m 15.36s
6	0.999 999	31.54s

I loaded up a conference room with all the people I thought we'd need. We had a great "mission specialist" present for each important aspect of the system, both functional and technical. We started the meeting around 3:00, thinking we'd be able to knock out our assignment by 5:00.

We got to four nines pretty easily. Back then, the technology was available to allow a really good team (and this was a really good team) to meet the requirement of not being down more than about 52 minutes a year. But we really got stymied when we thought about how to get from four nines to five. We knew how to reach 5 minutes of downtime a year, but we could not figure out how to do it without doubling the cost of a multimillion dollar system.

We rolled past 5:00, hoping for a eureka moment, but the eureka never came. We kept trying, but we just couldn't come up with an economical solution. Finally, around 7:00, we decided our only options were either to die in that room or surrender. I asked one of my teammates to see if Doug was still in the office. He was. Doug was awesome—his whole team was. I remember his face when he got to the door and saw all of us. "Wow," he said. "You guys look exhausted. What's up?"

We told him that we had a four-nines solution, but that we had proven to ourselves that there was no five-nines architecture that anyone could create at what we considered a reasonable cost. But, who knows, maybe his idea of a reasonable cost was different from ours.

He asked what the numbers were, and we told him. With no hesitation, he just said, "OK, four nines is good enough."

"Are you sure?" We all looked at each other like, can it possibly be this easy? "Yep, four nines is good enough. Anything else?"

We told him no, that was it. He thanked us for our hard work and bade us a good evening. The decision indeed was that easy with the decision-maker in the room, and Doug had the authority to make the decision. We should have called Doug at 5:00 that day instead of 7:00.

Shorten your feedback loop.

63

When Are You Done?

When are you finished optimizing? Oh, that's simple: you stop optimizing when further optimizing stops yielding sufficient benefit. But what does that *mean*?

One interpretation is that you're done optimizing when everyone who uses the system is happy with its performance. This interpretation has some commonsense appeal; it's harmonious with the old adage, "If it ain't broke, don't fix it."

But think about Kevin's invoicing story. What if they hadn't had a problem at month-end, and invoicing took forty seconds year-round? Would invoicing then have been "just fine," with no need to look at it any further? Even though Kevin's business was willing to consider a forty-second invoice creation "satisfactory," there was definitely business value to be had from improving it to less than a second.

Your standard of care should be better than just "everybody's happy." One reason is that happiness is subjective. Kevin's company was "happy" with forty-second invoicing only because they assumed it was impermissible to ask for anything better. What you need is an objective way to determine when you're done optimizing. And we have one:

Every important program should run at its "top speed."

Every program has a *top speed*, a speed at which your program cannot be made faster without changing its hardware. You have reached a program's top speed when:

1. It executes no unnecessary events (calls, instructions, etc.), and

2. Its events (calls, instructions, etc.) run at hardware speed.

That's it. Condition 1 means that your program is efficient, and condition 2 means that your program isn't waiting on anyone else. When you reach these conditions, the *only* way you'll be able to make your program go faster is to upgrade your hardware.

Once you know your program's top speed, you can make informed decisions like:

- How much would it be worth to the business *today*, in dollars, if this program could run closer to its top speed?

- How much would it be worth to the business *in the future* if this program could run closer to its top speed? For example, optimizing a program today might allow you to defer your hardware upgrade plans, improving your company's profit, cash flow, and return on investment.

- Does your requirement for how fast this program must run exceed its top speed? If it does, then there's no way you'll meet your requirements without an upgrade. This kind of thing, as you can imagine, is important to know.

It is important to understand that what is optimal from a software engineering perspective is not always optimal from a business perspective. The term *optimized* must ultimately be judged within the constraints of what the business is willing to pay for.

PART IX

Predicting

Richard

Richard (his real name) was the enterprise architect for a global convenience store chain, based in Irving, Texas. His company was having performance problems with a number of features in a new Oracle application they were rolling out. One feature in particular—a function called Material Specification Search—had become emblematic of the entire implementation. The company had purchased one of the most extraordinary computers on the planet, yet it would take nearly two minutes for a test kitchen chef to identify what kinds of cheeses were available for a new recipe.

By the time I met Richard on the phone in 2017, he had exhausted every avenue offered by the three international hardware, software, and consulting vendors with offices on site. He was eager to see what we might be able to do with our *look at it* approach. The night before our visit, I remember lying in bed thinking…my colleague Jeff Holt and I are going to be the first people in the world to learn why this search-for-cheese function is so slow.

Richard himself hosted the meeting the next morning. He was an ideal client:

- He had sufficient authority to provide access to anyone we needed: an application user who could reproduce the problem for us, a DBA to do the tracing and file fetching, and others as required.

- He had the authority to make decisions on behalf of his company.

- He was interested in how we worked, so he stayed right there with us, which kept our feedback loops short.

- He was a gracious host who, for example, kept bringing us store-branded snacks from the on-site store. When he figured out I liked ice cream, he brought ice cream every day I was there. He brought Jeff brownies.

As is often the case in our travels, the function was easy to trace, but the trace for just the user experience we were interested in was buried within several hundred trace files. It took Jeff a couple of hours to extract the data we needed. Since then, we've built software tools that would allow us to do the same job today in less than ten minutes.

The profile of the trace, aggregated by statement, was astonishing. Everyone in the room could suddenly answer not just the *how-long* question (nearly two minutes), but now, finally, the *why* question as well:

	Duration	
Statement	seconds	%
SELECT executions, end_of_fetch_count, elapsed_t...	97.676	88.6%
select gsmFormulaOutputTypeMML.Name from M...	4.862	4.4%
select gsmMaterialTypeMML.Name from MaterialS...	4.593	4.2%
SELECT Thumbnail, SpecNumber, SpecName, Shor...	2.089	1.9%
59 other statements	0.979	0.9%
Total (63)	110.200	100.0%

Almost 100 of the total 110 seconds of execution time were consumed by one statement, and *get this*: nobody in the room recognized the top statement—it wasn't part of the application! It was a feature interjected by the database to help make the other three statements faster. But the other three statements were already running just fine without the help, so we turned the feature off. Guess how much time that saved. It's the answer to the first *what-if* question.

If you guessed "about 97.676 seconds," then congratulations, you're today's lucky winner. Here's the new profile after shutting off the feature:

	Duration	
Statement	seconds	%
select gsmMaterialTypeMML.Name from MaterialS...	4.577	39.3%
select gsmFormulaOutputTypeMML.Name from M...	4.520	38.8%
SELECT Thumbnail, SpecNumber, SpecName, Shor...	2.175	18.7%
select default$ from col$ where rowid=:1	0.233	2.0%
27 other statements	0.141	1.2%
Total (31)	11.647	100.0%

Looking at it pays off, yet again.

At this point, the obvious next question is, *what else*? Are we done? A look at the new profile grouped by subroutine yields the answer:

Subroutine	Duration		Count	Mean
	seconds	%		
CPU: PARSE dbcalls	7.817	67.1%	881	0.008 873
SQL*Net message from client	1.689	14.5%	1,772	0.000 953
unaccounted-for between calls	1.078	9.3%	7,060	0.000 153
CPU: FETCH dbcalls	0.508	4.4%	2,490	0.000 204
10 other subroutines	0.555	4.8%	13,544	0.000 041
Total (14)	11.647	100.0%	25,747	0.000 452

We are in fact *not* done. Any good Oracle analyst should know that database PARSE operations should never dominate a profile. So then we have another iteration of our simple questions:

How long?

    11.6 seconds.

Why?

    Because of 881 PARSE dbcalls.

What if…

    we eliminate most of the parsing? We should eliminate nearly 8 seconds of PARSE calls, lots of network round trips, and lots of unaccounted-for time between calls. A rough guess would be that we could then search for materials in a second or two.

In Oracle, lots of time spent parsing is a sign that something is wrong with the way the application is written. Indeed, to fix this application would require us to rewrite it. We had, in the trace, all the information we needed to do it, but for the code we'd write to actually appear in the application would require cooperation from the application vendor.

It's a huge benefit to have access to a client decision-maker in situations like this. Richard had allocated nearly a whole week to the analysis of this Material Specification Search function, but it had taken us only a fraction of that time to reduce its response time from 110 seconds to 12 seconds. Richard therefore agreed that it would be interesting to see how quickly we could make it run. If it was a big enough improvement, he would champion the rewrite idea back with the application vendor.

The rewrite did in fact make a big difference:

Subroutine	Duration seconds	%	Count	Mean
SQL*Net message from client	0.472	53.8%	10	0.047 184
CPU: FETCH dbcalls	0.247	28.1%	542	0.000 456
CPU: EXEC dbcalls	0.140	16.0%	545	0.000 257
unaccounted-for between calls	0.008	0.9%	46	0.000 164
8 other subroutines	0.011	1.3%	2,243	0.000 005
Total (12)	0.877	100.0%	3,386	0.000 259

The impact was fantastic: from 110 seconds to 12 seconds, to less than one second. All we did was look at the right thing and eliminate unnecessary calls: first, by eliminating a statement that we just didn't need; and second, by rewriting the application to avoid a widely abused Oracle performance antipattern.

Are we done? Well, at this point, there wasn't much time left to get rid of. There were a few network round trips, which are probably inevitable. The database did a little work—also probably inevitable. And that's about it. There may have been a little bit more opportunity for improvement, but at this point, we had removed 90% of the function's execution time, and if the vendor would cooperate, that figure could become 99%. The answer to the *what-else* question at this point was to turn to the next problem on the list.

65

Why Predict?

If you could have any superpower, what would it be? Super speed? Super strength? X-ray vision? Invisibility? How about the ability to predict the future? Imagine knowing tomorrow's stock prices, who's going to win the next baseball game, what your opponent's next move is going to be. That might be fun.

Whereas most of the superpowers that I've listed here exist only in fantasy, the ability to predict is an actual skill that you can cultivate and improve with practice.

Predicting keeps you from wasting time and money on bad ideas.

People who are good predictors can fulfill bolder promises with less risk. They bring a huge competitive edge to the table.

66

Predicting with Profiles

Every *what-if* question is an appeal for a prediction. In Richard's story, what if you eliminate the statement that consumes 97 seconds? You should see 97 seconds less response time. What if you eliminate 800 parse calls? You'll spend almost 8 seconds less time parsing. Without a profile—armed, say, only with information that has been aggregated across lots of different programs—trying to answer simple questions like these can be maddening. But with a profile, answering such questions is not that difficult, even for people without a lot of experience.

The *fastest* way to become a better predictor is to use feedback:

1. Predict something. Try your best.

2. Execute and measure the phenomenon you tried to predict, and compare the measurements to your prediction. Learn which aspects of your prediction were correct and which were incorrect, so you can incorporate what you learn into your next prediction. Go to step 1.

The key is to predict results you can actually measure, so that you can compare your predictions head-to-head against what really happened. With enough practice, your predictions will become more and more reliable.

The fastest way to become a better predictor is to practice, with feedback.

67

Go/No-Go Predictions

Imagine that your TPS reports are slow, and that the profiles for all your TPS report executions look like this:

Event	Duration seconds	%	Count	Mean
disk read	1	0.1%	10	0.100
non-disk stuff	999	99.9%	4,990	0.200
Total	1,000	100.0%	5,000	0.200

Further imagine that your boss's plan for making TPS reports run faster is to buy an expensive new super-fast storage array that will make only "disk read" calls faster. What would you say?

I'm hopeful that you would be able to say confidently that buying a storage array to improve TPS reporting would be a horrible mistake (no matter how objectionable the mean duration of 0.100 sec/call may look). If the profile is accurate, then you can be 100.000% certain that faster storage access will not improve TPS report performance by any more than 0.1%.

You can make this binary go/no-go prediction without doing any arithmetic at all. Some of the predictions you'll make with profiles will be literally this easy. It's what *should* have happened before the Payroll users in Dallas did their CPU upgrade.

68

Linear Behavior

Imagine a profile as a spreadsheet, where the total duration for a line is the product of the execution count and the mean duration per execution:

	A	B	C	D
1	Event	Duration	Executions	Mean dur/exec
2	A	=C2*D2	?	?
3	B	=C3*D3	?	?
4	C	=C4*D4	?	?
5	Total	=SUM(B2:B4)	=SUM(C2:C4)	=B5/C5

This is an easy way to see why there are only two ways you can make something go faster:

- You can reduce an execution count (a value in column C); or
- You can reduce a mean duration per execution (a value in column D).

Because each value in column B is the product of its row-mates in columns C and D, it's easy to see what will happen if you change one of the input values. For example:

- If you multiply the value of cell C2 by 0.2, then the value of cell B2 will become 0.2 times its original value.
- If you cut D3 to 0.09 times its original value, then B3 will drop to 0.09 times its original value.
- If you multiply C4 by 0.50 and D4 by 0.33, then B4 will become 0.50×0.33 times its original value.

And of course, each of these changes will propagate into the sum in cell B5.

Predicting the answers to *what-if* questions this way is simple. The only trick is knowing what changes to make to the shaded region of the worksheet. Sometimes, because of skew, interdependencies, and queueing, the numbers you'll choose for your prediction may not be as obvious as you'd think.

69

Skew

Here's a profile for a program that took almost 22 hours to run:

Subroutine	Duration seconds	%	Count	Mean
single-block read	60,499	76.8%	10,013,394	0.006 042
other	18,290	23.2%	919,906	0.019 882
Total	78,789	100.0%	10,933,300	0.007 206

From this, you should be able to make some simple predictions:

1. How much time would you save if you could reduce the average "single-block read" call duration from 0.006 seconds to 0.004 seconds?
  You would save 10,013,394 calls × (0.006 − 0.004) sec/call ≈ 20,000 seconds.

2. How much time would you save if you could eliminate all 10,013,394 "single-block read" calls?
  You would save 60,499 seconds. Almost 17 hours.

3. How much time would you save if you could eliminate half of the "single-block read" calls?
  You would save half of 60,499 seconds, right? Actually…probably not. It *might* work out that way, but it's unlikely.

The snag is a data property called *skew*. Skew is nonuniformity in your data. A tidy little profile like the one I've shown here hides something important in that *mean* column: those ten million calls didn't all have the same duration. Some took a lot less than 0.006 seconds, and some took a lot more. How much time you save when you eliminate half your calls depends on *which* calls you eliminate.

Here is a profile showing "single-block read" calls grouped by duration. It's a histogram with 11 buckets:

	Range (seconds)		Duration		
	{min ≤ duration < max}		Seconds	%	Calls
1.	0.000 000	0.000 001			
2.	0.000 001	0.000 010	0	0.0%	15
3.	0.000 010	0.000 100	204	0.3%	9,345,811
4.	0.000 100	0.001 000	22	0.0%	108,181
5.	0.001 000	0.010 000	595	1.0%	103,462
6.	0.010 000	0.100 000	11,194	18.5%	315,149
7.	0.100 000	1.000 000	26,915	44.5%	133,382
8.	1.000 000	10.000 000	21,353	35.3%	7,375
9.	10.000 000	100.000 000	217	0.4%	19
10.	100.000 000	1,000.000 000			
11.	1,000.000 000	+∞			
Total (11)			60,499	100%	10,013,394

This table shows that even if you could eliminate every one of the more than 9 million calls in bucket 3, you would reduce the program's duration by only 204 seconds. On the other hand, if you could eliminate just the 133,382 calls in bucket 7, then you'd cut 26,915 seconds (7.5 hours). If you could eliminate the 7,375 calls in bucket 8, you'd cut 21,353 seconds (5.9 hours) more.

So then, how much time would you save if you could eliminate half of the "single-block read" calls? It depends on *which* calls you eliminate. In the worst case, if you happen to eliminate calls only in bucket 3, then you can eliminate over 93% of the calls but never make more than a 0.3% difference.[1] The best case would occur if you could eliminate calls in buckets 6–9, then you could make a 98.7% difference[2] by eliminating fewer than 5% of the calls.[3]

Remember, behind any aggregation (like "mean call duration"), there is a *list*. And until you know about the skew in that list, you have no idea how many of its elements bear any resemblance whatsoever to that average. That's why it's so nice to have the

---

1 (9,345,811 calls) / (10,013,394 calls) × 100% ≈ 93.3%.

2 (18.5 + 44.5 + 35.3 + 0.4)% = 98.7%.

3 36. (315,149 + 133,382 + 7,375 + 19) calls / (10,013,394 calls) × 100% ≈ 4.6%.

detail that a trace can give you. The right next move for this case would be to drill deeper into the data to see, first, what's special about the most time-consuming read calls and, second, how many of them you could remove.

70

Event Interdependencies

The events represented on the separate lines of a receipt-style profile can be inter-dependent. When you buy fewer wieners, you need fewer buns. When you visit your database buffer cache less often, you need fewer cache coherency instructions. Usually, the interdependency effect will work in your favor—you'll usually get more improvement than you expected when you eliminate event executions.

However, it's possible for interdependencies to work against you, too. When I buy less CoQ10, I need more Anacin©.

In my story about testing a program to learn its optimal fetch size, I hit the point of diminishing returns at 2,048. At this fetch size, my program was asking for more rows than would fit in a single network packet, and I began seeing calls to a new type of network I/O event that hadn't been part of the program's profile before. As I kept halving the number of fetch calls, the call count for this new network I/O event kept increasing. It was part of the reason that response times stopped getting better past 2,048.

Understanding the interdependencies among events will improve the accuracy of your predictions. You'll learn about your system's event interdependencies pretty quickly if you will always take the time to appraise your predictions and learn from your mistakes.

71

Nonlinear Behavior

Programs that queue a lot usually carry more opportunity for performance improvement than people tend to think. A few years ago, I wrote a program to demonstrate a common database application development mistake. To show how badly such a program could abuse a system, I simulated several users running this program all at the same time on a computer with very little CPU capacity. It spent most of its time queued for CPU:

Subroutine	Duration	Count	Mean
queued for CPU	**6.819**	**20,265**	0.000 336
other (CPU, disk, etc.)	4.782	50,295	0.000 095
Total	**11.601**	70,560	0.000 164

The point of my demonstration was that a simple modification to the source code would reduce the number of database calls (the requests that queue for CPU) from 20,000 to just 5,000. What do you think will happen to the "queued for CPU" duration if you were to make that modification?

A reasonable guess is that reducing the call count to 25% of its original value might reduce the duration to 25% of its original value, like this:

Subroutine	Duration	Count	Mean
queued for CPU (predicted)	**1.705**	**5,066**	**0.000 336**
	0.25×6.819	$0.25 \times 20,265$	

But in reality, reducing the call count to 25% of its original value reduced the duration to just 11% of its original value:

Subroutine	Duration	Count	Mean
queued for CPU (actual)	0.769	5,003	0.000 154

OK, that's great news, but why did it happen that way?

The prediction was wrong because it didn't account for the fact that reducing the call count would also reduce the mean duration per call, which dropped from 0.000 336 seconds to 0.000 154 seconds. Before modifying the source code, the combined effect of high call counts and high concurrency had added queueing delays to the call response times. Reducing the call count for each execution reduced our traffic intensity, which moved us down the hyperbolic ski slope to a lower response time per call.

Let's look at another example to get a better feel for what's going on. Imagine an M/M/2 system with traffic intensity $\rho = 0.9$, and the average queueing delay $Q = 4.26\ S$ (that is, 4.26 service times). What would you expect to happen if you could reduce the traffic intensity by 1/3? Your intuition probably tells you that reducing traffic intensity by 1/3 should reduce queueing delay by 1/3. Exercising this intuition would yield the prediction $Q = 4.26\ S \times (1 - 1/3) = 2.84\ S$. But, in actual fact, the queueing delay at $\rho = 0.6$ is significantly better than that; it turns out to be $Q = 0.56\ S$.

Here's the picture. Note that it's a plot of just Q, not R:

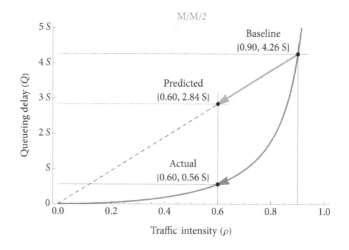

The prediction that Q will improve proportionally with ρ assumes that the trajectory of the improvement is a line from the baseline at $(0.90, 4.26\ S)$ to the origin at $(0, 0)$. But the actual trajectory of the system's behavior from the baseline to the origin is a hyperbola that plummets much more rapidly than the line does. It is *superlinear*—better than linear—improvement.

So, when you add load to a busy system (even just a little bit), response times decay hyperbolically, which is awful. But it also happens that when you reduce a heavy workload—even just a little bit!—response times *improve* hyperbolically, which is fantastic. At high loads, the hyperbola caused by queueing magnifies the impact of everything you do, whether it's good *or* evil.

Predicting nonlinear improvements can be hard. M/M/c is a nice model for some systems or subsystems you'll encounter, but the model is not sophisticated enough to cover you on predicting the behavior of more complicated systems. That's why you should always *test* your predictions. The higher the stakes, the more important testing becomes.

The general shape of the curve, however, is important to understand. It helps you understand why a little bit of attention to eliminating wasted workload can have a better-than-expected effect upon response times.

Eliminating wasteful work at high loads can improve performance faster than you might have expected.

PART X

Latency Hiding

Mom

Here's a sequence diagram for preparing dinner:

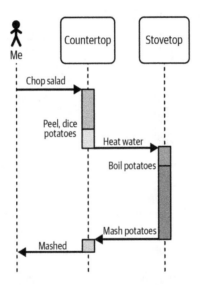

It'll get dinner done, but it's not a smart way to do it. My mom taught me a better way. It was the way her mom taught her. It starts with: hey, don't chop the salad first; put the water on the stove first. It takes a while for the water to boil. When it finally does, you need the potatoes to be ready to go in. So, while the water is warming up, don't chop the salad; peel and dice the potatoes. When your potatoes are in the water, *then* chop the salad.

Why did my mom teach me to do it this particular way? To save time. There's no sense sitting around twiddling your fingers while the potatoes are boiling. And there's no sense letting the stove sit there idle while it could be getting work done. My mom and my grandmother were *not* finger-twiddling idlers, I can assure you. They were latency assassins.

Here's a picture that shows why it saves time to take the "chop salad" step off the critical path:

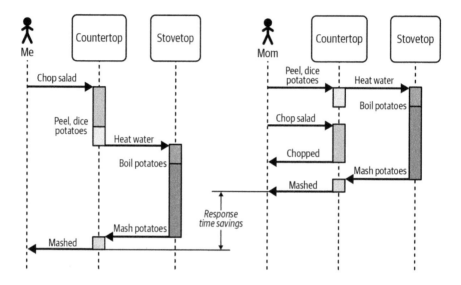

Chopping the salad while the potatoes are boiling is a technique called *latency hiding*. If you google it, you'll find lots of complicated technical papers, but latency hiding is just the act of saving time by hiding durations behind other durations.

I also learned a lot about latency hiding as a kid playing golf with adults. There's a lot of preparation involved in making a golf shot, things like:

- Find your ball.
- Calculate the distance from your ball to the hole.
- Choose the shape of the shot you'll attempt.
- Choose your club.
- Choose your line.
- Take a practice swing or two.

In golf, you're expected to have done all these things before it becomes your turn to hit your shot. So you hide the latency of all these activities that you can (subject to your not bothering someone else), *before* it's your turn, while your playing partners are hitting their shots. If you don't learn to be ready to hit your shot when it's your turn, then people stop wanting you in their group.

You've probably built latency hiding into your life already. It's what you're doing when you:

- Watch a movie during your flight.
- Use the bathroom during your game's commercial breaks.
- Read GL trial balance reports during your visit to the men's room.
- Check your email during your conference call.
- Wash your windshield while your car is filling up.
- Make a hands-free phone call during your drive home from work.
- Marvel at scenic Nepal as you await your seat on Expedition Everest™.
- Tell your audience a story while your demo script runs.
- Run your backup at midnight when nobody cares how long it takes.

Once you start thinking about it, you'll find opportunities for latency hiding everywhere you look.

73

Dominic

At the Oracle OpenWorld conference of September 1994, I was in the Moscone Center audience of a beautifully performed presentation by Oracle CEO Larry Ellison. On stage with Larry were two lecterns, each with a keyboard and a terminal. Behind him were three giant screens. The leftmost lectern and the screen behind it were for Larry in the role of Application User. The rightmost lectern and the screen behind it were for Larry in the role of DBA. Between the lecterns was an exciting new nCUBE computer. We'd heard of the nCUBE, but none of us had ever seen one before. Both lecterns were connected to it. The third screen, positioned between the other two screens, showed a utilization graph for the nCUBE's CPUs. I think this demo model had 64 CPUs. It might have had a lot more.

Larry began his demo at the User lectern. He showed us a complicated SQL query that he said would take (if I recall correctly) about 2 minutes and 35 seconds to run. Then he ran the query. While it ran, he told us that the reason it took so long was that it needed to scan and process a lot of data. While he was telling his story, the nCUBE computer's CPU monitor in the middle showed one red bar of solid CPU activity for the duration of the query. He finished his story just in time to gesture toward his screen on the left. Right on cue, his User screen displayed the query result, along with the news that it had consumed 2:35. Simultaneously, the red bar on the CPU monitor went background black.

Larry then walked across the stage to the DBA lectern. He explained that executing the query in parallel would dramatically reduce this query's response time, especially with this nCUBE, which—with its many CPUs—had just an outrageous capacity for parallel processing. But he told us that, although the machine had this enormous capacity going unused, parallelizing the application might be difficult. It would require a reimagining of the application, followed by rewriting, retesting, and so on. Most companies would be reluctant to do all this work, and the companies who had bought their applications from someone else wouldn't even have the choice.

He then proceeded to explain a new Oracle Database feature called Oracle Declarative Parallel Execution, which would allow him—as a DBA with *no* access whatsoever to the application code—to run the 2:35 query in parallel. At the DBA lectern, he altered a new degree-of-parallelism property on the main table that the application was reading. Then he walked back to the User lectern and re-executed the exact same 2:35 query as before. He didn't retype it. He just reran it.

But this time was different. Instead of just one red bar on the center screen, all of its bars went bright red. It was like a video of the sun exploding. I kidded people later that we should have brought welding goggles. But it lasted for only a second or two before the bars went black again. The screen on the left displayed the query result (the same answer as before), along with the news that the query had consumed just 2 seconds or something like that.

Larry said when you've got all these CPUs, you might as well use them! The audience erupted into applause. I could tell that just about everyone in the room was imagining this new parallel execution feature as the cure for all their performance problems. My friend Dominic sitting next to me leaned over and said exactly what I was thinking: "Yeah. It *would* be nice to have an nCUBE all to myself…"

74

Parallelization

Parallelization is a form of latency hiding. It works like this:

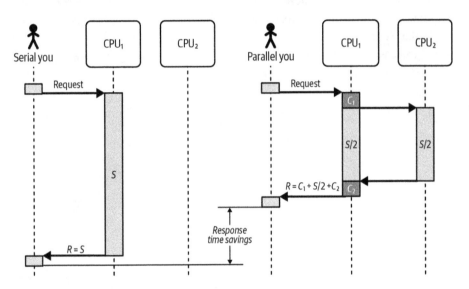

The point of parallelizing a task is to reduce that task's response time by exploiting unused capacity. However, the benefits of parallelization come at a cost. Parallel operations can reduce response times, but they don't reduce load. Parallelizing in fact always increases system load, because parallel algorithms require extra instructions to partition the workload among the parallel processes and then harvest the work done by those processes (the extra C1 and C2 costs in my sequence diagram above).

Parallel algorithms can have false allure. For example, imagine a serial algorithm that returns its result in 10 seconds, using 10 seconds' worth of resources. Now imagine a parallel algorithm that returns the same result in 5 seconds, but it consumes

50 seconds' worth of resources. The parallel algorithm will be alluring to its user because it's twice as fast, but it will put five times more load onto the system.

If just one person on the system uses the parallel algorithm, the resulting increase in traffic intensity, crammed into one little 5-second interval, might go unnoticed. But when everyone else gets wind that they can cut their response times in half by parallelizing their stuff, too, traffic intensities can grow quickly to the point where everyone is miserable, high and right on the response time hyperbola.

The ability to operate in parallel is a nice tool to have, especially for long, scheduled jobs that crunch along, say, at night when the system is mostly idle. There's nothing wrong with parallelizing a big batch job to take advantage of the otherwise unused CPUs. But using parallel operations on a high-concurrency interactive system can be treacherous. For example, letting 1,000 users parallelize their work into 8 concurrent threads is like adding 7,000 users to your system.

75

How to Melt a System

In 2012, I joined a group of colleagues for a course about a new type of system called the Oracle Exadata Database Machine. The Exadata machine had been engineered specifically to be the best-performing Oracle hardware platform on Earth. It was. The engineers at Oracle had not just selected all the best hardware components, they had integrated the Oracle Database software into the hardware in a unique and elegant way.

For example, the engineers of course chose an absurdly fast interconnect for communication between the database compute nodes and the associated storage nodes. But even better, they pushed Oracle Database code that does data filtering (implementing a SQL query's *where* clause) down into the storage array. Now instead of transporting whole database blocks (typically 4,096 or 8,192 bytes apiece) to the compute nodes, which would then filter out (discard) any unwanted rows, the storage arrays would send just the rows the compute nodes wanted. This smart idea can reduce traffic intensity on the interconnect by two or three orders of magnitude. There were lots of pleasant high-efficiency surprises like this in the machine.

All of us in the course already had a lot of Oracle experience, and so we finished the instructor's exercises pretty quickly. This left us some extra time to experiment. One of the things we wanted to see was how this extraordinary system would behave under duress, so we decided to play a little game of "melt the system." The game here is to add so much load that we start seeing performance problems. Then we keep adding load until the system basically can't function anymore (on the vertical slope of the queueing delay hyperbola). We'd then know how these new machines would act in the wild under conditions of too much workload.

So how would we melt one of these engineered Oracle systems? This thing could accommodate tens of thousands of users and had tremendous defenses built in to handle the toughest workloads.

Well, one way to do it is to write a little program to connect to the database instance, execute some little transaction, and then disconnect. There are probably plenty of examples online of little Java programs that could do that. We could each call such a program bazillions of times from a loop in a shell script, using the shell's & operator to force work into the background so we could keep heaping more concurrent program executions onto the system. We could have done that in the classroom, in probably a half hour or so.

But we chose an easier way to bring this huge machine to its knees. We simply created a huge table (easy to do in SQL), and we declared Oracle's parallel degree for that new table to be 256. Then, every time a student queried this big table, Oracle would create 512 new database processes.[1] That was plenty of load to melt the system. Using parallel execution features is an easy way to add load to a system, whether that's your intention or not.

It's not a bug; it's how parallelization is *meant* to work. It's *designed* to use every bit of resource you'll let it use, to optimize one user's experience, potentially at the expense of everything and everybody else. It is incumbent upon the managers of a system to prevent people from abusing it. "Too much of a good thing," as they say, "can kill you."

---

1 Oracle uses a producer–consumer model that spawns *two* processes (sometimes more) per declared parallel degree.

76

Multitasking

Have you ever wondered how a computer with more users than CPUs can serve all of you "at once"? The answer is a scheduling algorithm called *preemptive multitasking*. It works like this…

Imagine that you and one friend are the only users on a computer with one single-core CPU. Each of you wants to execute a program requiring 2 seconds of CPU time. You make your request at time 0, and she makes hers 1 second later, at time 1, while your program is running:

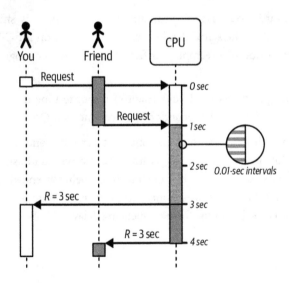

When you run your program at time 0, the CPU is idle, so it begins executing your program's instructions right away. Every 1/100th of a second,[1] the CPU sends a *scheduler interrupt* to the operating system, telling it to stop executing the currently running program and instead run an operating system subroutine called the *scheduler*. With no other program waiting in the queue, the scheduler simply passes control of the CPU back to your program. Then, 1/100th of a second later, the same thing happens again.

Your program receives CPU service in this manner until the first scheduler interrupt after your friend runs her program at time 1. The scheduler then finds your friend's program in the run queue and executes a procedure called a *context switch*, which switches your program to the run queue for waiting, and your friend's program to the CPU for execution. Your friend proceeds to get 1/100th of a second of CPU service until the next scheduler interrupt.

This interrupting and switching continues, with each of you getting half a second of CPU per second until your program finishes at time 3.

From time 3 onward, your friend's program runs by itself. It is still interrupted 100 times per second by the scheduler, but with no competition for CPU in the run queue, the scheduler doesn't preempt your friend again, and her program finishes at time 4.

After all this, your program's (and your friend's) response time is 3 seconds: that's 1 second of queueing delay, and 2 seconds of service time ($R = Q + S = 1 + 2 = 3$).

Machines these days have more than just one core per CPU, and many have more than one CPU. But fundamentally, this is how preemptive multitasking works. It's how computers make all of us feel like our needs are being attended to, even when there's more demand than there are resources to serve it all. Who pays for it? All the system's users pay a little bit, in the form of queueing delay.

---

1 The frequency is configurable. On most systems it is 100 times per second.

77

Human Multitasking

A computer uses preemptive multitasking to create the illusion that the machine is devoting all of its attention to you. The principle works beautifully, as long as the scheduler doesn't take too long to do things like figure out which process in the run queue should run next, pack up the program that's on the CPU, and load the program being scheduled.

And that's why preemptive multitasking works fine for computers but not for people: a computer context switch takes a few microseconds, but human context switches take about 25 minutes. They're expensive in more ways than just wasted time:[1]

> *...Research has also found that multitasking contributes to the release of stress hormones and adrenaline, which can cause long-term health problems if not controlled, and contributes to the loss of short-term memory.*

In other words, trying too hard to do more than one thing at once literally makes you sick, and it makes you stupid. If you want high performance from yourself, don't multitask. Leave that to the machines.

---

1 Christine Rosen, "The Myth of Multitasking." *The New Atlantis*, Spring 2008, *https://oreil.ly/EX1SP*.

PART XI

Fallacies

78

The Evil Genie

One of the most insidious problems you can have is when something's wrong, but your tools tell you everything's fine. "My users *must* be happy, because my CPU utilization is in the green zone!" Well, that statement might sound sensible, but the "because" part just isn't true. This problem is an example of a more general problem of surrogacy—it's asking for something (green-zone CPU utilization) that's not really the same as what you want (happy users).

To help me teach this lesson, I like to introduce my friend, the *evil genie*. Think of Elizabeth Hurley in *Bedazzled*, or just about any episode of *The Twilight Zone*. The formula is that you make a wish, and then the genie grants it—but it doesn't turn out the way you want. For example, "I just want people to leave me alone," makes you the sole survivor of a nuclear holocaust. That kind of thing.

The tools you use can trick you the same way, even when they're not lying to you. They can do it simply by measuring the wrong things. The solution is straightforward: just be careful what you wish for. The *test* is to imagine "Could an evil genie grant my wish without giving me what I really want?" What you're really asking is, "Could this measurement tool trick me into having false beliefs about my system?"

There are many ways a genie—or a well-intended measurement tool—can make an activity *appear* beneficial without actually accomplishing anything useful. Progress can be especially illusory when you're working with ratios. The scary part is that almost *all* of the performance metrics people are accustomed to looking at...*are* ratios. Let's explore.

79

The Leather Jacket

One cool autumn day, I walked into the office wearing a brand-new leather jacket that my wife had helped me pick out the night before at the outlet mall. A friend complimented me and asked—if I didn't mind telling—how much that new jacket cost.

I told him I'd paid a hundred dollars for it.

"A hundred dollars!" That seemed to excite him, "I have a jacket nearly just like that—it may not be as nice as the one you're wearing—and it cost me *three times* that much!"

Hearing that made me pleased that I bought the jacket my wife had recommended, even though I'd been nervous about it in the store.

Then he said, knowing that I would know what he meant, "I think I'll go buy myself one of those tonight. It'll bring my average price per jacket down to just two hundred dollars. Then, I'll feel better about myself."

80

The Buried Outlier

Something like this is eventually going to happen to you:

You: "Your order entry program was slow on Wednesday because it executed a single 512-byte write call that took 18.6 seconds."

Businessperson: "Oh wow, I'll share that information with our storage administrator!"

Storage administrator: "No, that's impossible. We couldn't have had an 18.6-second single-block write call. Our average write latency on Wednesday was 0.001 seconds."

You: "Well, the *pwrite* call is in the program's trace. It completed Wednesday at 14:02:28.176910 and took 18.582771 seconds."

SA: "That couldn't have happened. Your trace is wrong."

Yet your trace is correct. How is that possible?

There are lots of ways it could have happened. For example, if there were a million *pwrite* calls on Wednesday, and every call took 0.001 seconds apiece except for the one that took 18.6 seconds, then the average would be 0.001 019 seconds per call.[1] In a million calls, you can bury *five* 18.6-second outliers without increasing the average by even a tenth of a millisecond.[2]

It's easy for outliers to get buried, especially in really long lists, so just because a number seems implausible doesn't mean it didn't happen.

---

1 ((1 call) × 18.6 (seconds/call) + (1,000,000 − 1) calls × 0.001(seconds/call)) / 1,000,000 calls ≈ 0.001 019 seconds/call.

2 ((5 calls) × 18.6 (seconds/call) + (1,000,000 − 5) calls × 0.001(seconds/call)) / 1,000,000 calls ≈ 0.001 093 seconds/call.

81

Be Careful What You Wish For

Sometimes, you just need to take a walk with your customer and talk through what you're really trying to accomplish. One time, on one such walk, I asked an IT director with a slow system what he *really* hoped to achieve from my consulting visit. He said, "To be honest with you, what I really want is to have my CPUs be at least 40% idle during my peak-load hour every afternoon."

I told him I understood what he meant, but that lower CPU utilization wasn't really what he wanted. Of course, this was a plot twist for him. Why would that not be what he really wanted?

I explained that it's the wrong goal, because there are ways I could give him what he's asking for, without giving him anything that he actually wants. For instance, I asked him if he had any slow, really old disk drives in a storage closet somewhere. I said that if we could install those really slow disk drives, it would reduce his CPU utilization, which would meet his *stated* goal, but it wouldn't give him what he really wanted.

You always risk wasting your time if you don't look at the right "it."

The following sequence diagram shows why. Slower disks would cause more CPU idle time, which would officially fulfill his wish. But it would come at the expense of making his programs take longer, which is counter to what he really wants.

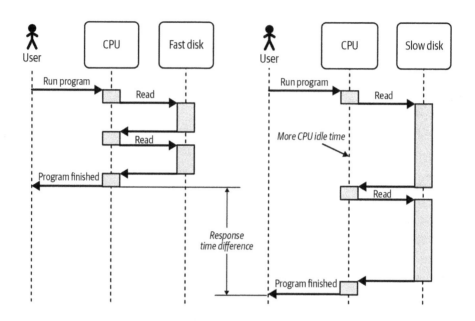

With slow enough drives (paper tape, anyone?!), I could give him all the idle CPU that he could ever want. Not that I would, of course, but playing the evil genie game proves an important point. By demonstrating a way to fulfill the letter of a wish without fulfilling its intent, you prove how it's possible for your users to be suffering while a measurement you're looking at is green.

Of course, it was never a particular CPU utilization number that he really wanted; utilization was only an easy-to-measure side effect. What he really wanted was for his peak-hour programs to run efficiently and finish more quickly. The feedback he needed for measuring progress against that goal was a measure of how long people's program executions were taking and why.

He admitted that it was obvious, once I said it out loud. But he had been conditioned to believe that such measurements were impossible to obtain. Of course, those measurements aren't impossible to obtain—you can get them by tracing.

82

Percentile Specifications

Imagine there's a task that you execute on your computer hundreds of times every day. And let's imagine that your tolerance for this task's duration is 5 seconds per execution, so you formally agree with your application service provider that you'll be officially satisfied as long as the average response time for this task is 5 seconds or less.

But the first day you use the application, you don't feel very good about it. You formally object. And so the vendor looks up the numbers for a ten-run period you agreed is representative of why you feel bad about performance. It's no wonder you're upset. You circle all the cells where your expectations weren't met, and you find out that you were disappointed with half the experiences—5 out of 10.

Response time (seconds)										Average
1	(8)	(6)	2	1	(10)	1	(9)	5	(7)	5.0

"But," your service provider insists, "you must agree that we're meeting your official average response time requirement of 5 seconds or less." Yes, in fact the average is 5.0 seconds exactly. But you're not happy, so apparently what you *thought* you wanted was not what you *really* wanted.

So, your vendor—benevolently—offers a new type of agreement. "You seem concerned about how often you're disappointed, so let's come to an agreement on how often you're willing to be disappointed." You agree with the format, and you choose the number 10% as your disappointment threshold. As long as no more than 10% of your executions finish in more than 5 seconds, you'll be satisfied.

But on the second day you use the application, you don't feel that much better. So you open a new complaint. Here are the second day's numbers:

Response time (seconds)										Average	Percentile
1	1	1	1	1	1	(41)	1	1	1	5.0	90% @ ≤5.0

OK, the ones are great, but that 41-second experience was so long that you remember wondering whether the system was down. You got a cup of coffee, and when you got back, the execution had completed. For numbers like 41 to occur in 1 out of 10 executions isn't going to work, either.

You finally realize that what you really want is a system that usually responds in less than 5 seconds, and that almost never responds in more than about 10 seconds. It's impossible to guarantee *never*, but you can negotiate how often you'll tolerate numbers bigger than 10. Of course, your vendor has a right to remind you that the more you ask for, the more you'll have to pay, so you'll need to strike a balance. You end up mutually agreeing on the following service level:

- Response time must be 5 seconds or less in at least 90% of executions, and
- Response time must be 10 seconds or less in at least 99% of executions.

These constraints are called *percentile specifications*. They allow you to specify mathematical constraints on how much variation you'll tolerate. This two-level deep percentile specification is a good way to help you say what kind of performance you really want.

83

The Hit Rate Problem

Several years ago, the Oracle world—followed by the MySQL world and some other worlds as well—underwent a cultural shift in how people measured performance. It was a shift away from judging the performance of a system based primarily upon a metric called the *cache hit ratio*.

The Oracle Database product uses a shared memory structure called the *database buffer cache*. It's where Oracle sessions manage database blocks that they've read recently from the operating system. Finding a block in the buffer cache (a cache hit) is quicker and less expensive than not finding it (a cache miss). When the block that an Oracle session needs is not in the buffer cache, it takes extra instructions, including an operating system read call, to put it there.

The cache hit ratio (CHR) is the ratio of hits to attempts. Since Oracle directly measures misses instead of hits, people calculate hits as attempts minus misses $(a - m)$, yielding the formula CHR $= (a - m)/a$. For example:

Attempts (a)	Misses (m)	Hits $(a - m)$	Hit ratio $((a - m)/a)$
100	0	100	100.0%
100	30	70	70.0%
100	100	0	0.0%
10,392	572	9,820	94.5%

A ratio defined this way seems like a perfectly obvious higher-is-better metric. For example, imagine that SQL statements A and B both return identical results. Which statement would you want to use?

Measure	SQL A	SQL B
Attempts	100	100
Misses	10	1
Hits	90	99
Hit rate	90%	99%

The right answer is SQL B, because its execution has fewer misses with the same number of attempts. It does the same job with less work. In Oracle, sometimes you can create a result like this just by allocating more memory to the buffer cache to increase the hit count, without changing the SQL at all. It was so easy to do that a lot of people did it, and it helped some of them.

But most people overlooked another important situation. I can remember one of my early Oracle mentors showing me this situation at a chalkboard. Imagine this time that statements C and D both return the same answer. So then, which of *these* two statements would you want to use?

Measure	SQL C	SQL D
Hit rate	99.9%	80%

The statement C hit rate is obviously better, with its much-better hit ratio, so how could there be any question?

But if you look at the data behind the ratios, you find out that C is the wrong answer. And not just a little wrong. Outrageously wrong.

Measure	SQL C	SQL D
Attempts	1,000,000	10
Misses	1,000	2
Hits	999,000	8
Hit rate	99.9%	80%

Statement D is 10,000 times more efficient, because it delivers the same results with far less work, in spite of its hit rate looking orders of magnitude worse.

So then, is hit rate a higher-is-better metric, or not?

It is, in fact, *not*. This is not just an academic exercise. There were thousands of system managers out there who had loads of undetected, poor-performing SQL on their systems because they had chosen an unreliable metric as their primary feedback measurement. It wasn't their fault, by the way; they were just doing what they had been *taught* to do.

My friend Connor McDonald published a program in 2001 called `choose_a_hit_ratio`, which let you increase your database buffer cache hit rate to any value you liked between your current value and 0.999 999 999. It worked as advertised. It simply executed an appropriately enormous number of unnecessary hits upon the database buffer cache.

It printed the following warning, which says pretty much everything you need to know:[1]

```
*******************************************************************
                            WARNING
Responding affirmatively to the following prompt will create the
following effects:
1) It will degrade the performance of your database while it runs.
2) It might run a very long time.
3) It will "improve" your system's buffer cache hit ratio.
4) It will prove that a high database buffer cache hit ratio is
   an unreliable indicator of Oracle system performance.
*******************************************************************
```

One of my database administrator friends and I had a laugh-out-loud moment together after I presented at a conference about the hit rate fallacy. He told me that his compensation plan included a buffer cache hit ratio component. The higher he could make his systems' buffer cache hit ratios, the more he got paid! Connor's program might as well be a printing press for cash! Theoretically, anyway. My friend told us that the bonus pool hadn't really been that big lately.

We agreed that maybe we could kind of see why.

This is an Oracle story, but the problem is not just an Oracle problem. Nor is it just a hit rate problem. It's a problem with ratios in general.

---

1 Millsap and Holt, *Optimizing*, 365–371.

84

The MPG Problem

The hit rate fallacy is a problem with ratios in general. For this story, let's use an automotive metric with which you're probably already intimate: *miles per gallon* (*mpg*). The mpg metric is defined simply as the number of miles you drive divided by the number of gallons of fuel that you burn. It's an efficiency metric. More efficiency is always good, so it makes sense that mpg is a higher-is-better metric. But, as innocent as a simple "output divided by input" ratio sounds, even *efficiency* itself is indeed susceptible to ratio fallacies.

Imagine that there are two distinct routes to your office at work: call them A and B. When you take route A, your fuel efficiency is 20 mpg. On route B, your mileage is 30 mpg. Which route should you choose? It seems an easy choice: more efficiency is better, and 30 mpg is more than 20 mpg, so then 30 mpg is better. Therefore, obviously, route B is better. It's just common sense.

Except, well…it's the wrong answer. Let's look at what's really going on:

Measure	Route A	Route B
Distance	5 miles	20 miles
Duration	10 minutes	25 minutes
Fuel burned	0.25 gallons	0.67 gallons
Notes	Stop-and-go city driving	Steady freeway driving
Fuel efficiency	20 mpg	30 mpg

So, which route should you take? It's obvious when you look at more facts: route A is 15 miles shorter, 15 minutes faster, and uses nearly half a gallon less fuel. Route A is the superior route.

That's right: route A, with the worse mpg figure, is better. *Vastly* better. But the metric designed *specifically for measuring efficiency* says that route B is more efficient. What in the world is going on?!

85

The Ratio Trick

I've played the same evil genie trick in both the Oracle buffer cache hit ratio story, and the mpg story. And I can play it for any ratio you want, even throughput and response time! Here's the trick.[1] Any ratio (r) is the quotient of a numerator (n) and a denominator (d): $r = n/d$. You probably remember two ways to make a ratio's value bigger:

a. You can make the numerator (n) bigger; or

b. You can make the denominator (d) smaller.

Option b is always a good move for higher-is-better metrics, because the denominator represents a cost that you want to reduce. In the Oracle story, the denominator was the number of attempts upon the buffer cache. Eliminating attempts reduces the amount of work that the machine has to do, which frees up resources and makes the system run better. In the mpg story, the denominator was the amount of fuel consumed. Of course, the less fuel you consume, the better.

Option a—making the numerator bigger—is a sneaky option. In a higher-is-better metric, the numerator represents the good thing that you want more of....Except when you have all you want of your good thing, and you don't need any more. In the Oracle story, we wanted more cache hits for a given attempt count. If making the cache bigger accomplishes that, then it's a win for the system. But you don't need a bunch of extra hits caused by the choose_a_hit_ratio program, putting an extra burden on the system just to pad the hit rate.

---

1 I'll show it to you for higher-is-better metrics. It's the same principle for lower-is-better metrics.

Likewise, in the mpg story, you didn't really want to go 20 miles; you only wanted to go 5. By packing the numerator with miles you didn't really want to drive, my evil genie gave you a better-looking efficiency metric value, but you actually ended up wasting time and burning more fuel:

Measure	Route A	Route B
Distance	5 miles	20 miles
Duration	10 minutes	25 minutes
Fuel burned	0.25 gallons	0.67 gallons
Notes	Stop-and-go city driving	Steady freeway driving
Fuel efficiency	20 mpg	30 mpg

Here's something interesting: burning more fuel on the 20-mile route *increased* the denominator in mpg = m/g. Shouldn't that have *reduced* your mpg ratio? Making g bigger should have made mpg smaller. The reason it didn't is because the evil genie who made up route B *cheated*. I didn't just make the denominator (gallons) bigger; I made the numerator (miles) bigger, too.

It turns out, there aren't just two ways to make a ratio bigger; there's actually a *third*:

    c. You can make both the numerator (n) and denominator (d) bigger, as long as you grow n by a bigger factor than you grow d.

And that—option *c*—is the evil genie trick I played on you in both stories. In the Oracle story, I packed both the hit and attempt counts, but I grew h faster than a:

Measure	Good SQL	Bad SQL	Growth factor
Hits (h)	8	999,000	124,875
Attempts (a)	10	1,000,000	100,000
Hit rate (h/a)	0.8	0.999	1.25

In the mpg story, I packed both the distance and the fuel burned, but I grew the distance faster than I grew the fuel consumption:

Measure	Good route	Bad route	Growth factor
Miles (m)	5 miles	20 miles	4.0
Gallons (g)	0.25 gal	0.67 gal	2.7
mpg (m/g)	20 mpg	30 mpg	1.5

86

Even Throughput and Response Time?

A smart evil genie can game *any* ratio. Even throughput and response time. Come on, I'll show you how.

Throughput is output divided by a duration. To make your throughput look better than it really is, all she has to do is add a bunch of really fast-completing task executions to your load. These executions don't even have to do anything useful; they could even create positive harm. It doesn't matter. The only constraint is that they just have to count as executions. All she has to do is increase the completion count for whatever duration you're using, and now you're looking at a higher-is-better throughput metric value that got bigger, and therefore "better," but by making your system worse off—by leaving you with a higher traffic intensity.

Now, let's do response time. Is that even a ratio? Yes it is: it's a duration divided by a count of task executions. When you're looking at the response time of a single execution, you don't give the evil genie much room to maneuver. But if you start aggregating response times, oh, that's all the help she needs! If she wants your average response times to look better without actually making your system better, all she has to do is introduce a gazillion short-duration task executions (whether anybody wants the output of those executions or not). This will reduce the *reported* average response time for everyone. But the actual experiences that your users feel will be worse, because the system is busier doing evil genie work now.

You can game any ratio. Even throughput and response time.

87

Are Ratios Useless?

Are all ratios just fundamentally unreliable? Are they useless? If they are, then what are you supposed to look at instead? What metrics should you use to drive your feedback loop?

The short answer is, ratios are not useless, but any time you see one, you need to regard it with suspicion. When you see a ratio improve, dig into the numerator and the denominator to find out whether it improved for a reason that's good for your system.

Too much trust in ratios makes you susceptible to evil genie shenanigans. As I showed in the Oracle and mpg stories, following even perfectly sensible ratios can lead to bad decisions. There's no evil intent required. The evil genie metaphor is just a device for showing you that if you're not careful about what you ask for, you might not get what you want.

So, when can you rely on a ratio for decision making? My advice is to look at the numbers that make up a ratio before you look at the ratio's value itself. Unless you can see the values that make up a ratio, you can't trust it. One of my favorite authors, the late Clayton Christensen, said, "I've never seen a bank that accepts deposits in ratios."

Don't rely solely on ratios for decision making.

88

When Ratios Are Reliable

Ratios become *reliable* metrics for comparing two systems (or two system states) if you first eliminate all the waste from the ratios you are comparing. In the Oracle story, if you focus first on eliminating wasteful buffer cache accesses, then you'll never get tricked by the evil genie who padded your numerator and denominator by almost a million apiece to give you a 0.999 hit rate.[1] In the mpg story, if you first eliminate the wasteful distance, then you'll never get tricked into thinking that the better mpg route is the better overall route.

But identifying waste isn't always as simple as it sounds. Let's examine that for a minute, going back to the mpg story. Imagine there's a third route called C that is six miles long, on which you can get 30 mpg. You've already seen that you can't just say route C is superior because of its better mpg score. But is it possible that this new longer route C could be better than the shorter route A? Let's see:

Measure	Route A	Route C	Growth factor
Distance (miles)	5	6	1.2
Fuel burned (gallons)	0.25	0.20	0.8
Duration (minutes)	10	8	0.8
Fuel mileage (mpg)	20	30	1.5

This route C is indeed an improvement over route A in two important regards: even though the route is longer, it gets you to work 2 minutes sooner, and it burns 0.05 gallons less fuel. Is it tire and engine wear that you're concerned about? Route C

---

1 When you see a hit rate with lots of nines in it, realize that you can't have *n* nines in your hit rate unless you have at least *n* + 1 digits in your attempts count.

is slightly longer than route A, but the highway driving may actually be a little easier on your car.

When you optimize, think about what you really want more of. List the attributes of the experience that you really care about. Then make the trade-offs that will create the best results.

89

Describing Performance Improvements

Once I saw an ad claiming that a product could improve response times by 1,000%. Sounds great. But what does that mean?

Here are two ways to express response time improvements:

What proportion of the time did you save?
  $p = (old - new)/old$. It's the improvement expressed as a proportion of the *old* value. You can multiply p by 100% if you want, to express it as a percentage.[1]

How many times faster is it now?
  That's $n = old/new$. Don't express this number as a percentage. It's not helpful to the recipient of the information.

Here are some examples:

Before (old)	After (new)	"p% faster" (p = (old − new)/old × 100%)	"n times faster" (n = old/new)
60 sec	60 sec	0.0%	1
60 sec	59 sec	1.7%	1.017
60 sec	20 sec	66.7%	3
60 sec	1 sec	98.3%	60
60 sec	0 sec	100.0%	+∞

---

1 ...Because "%" is a symbol whose value is 0.01, so 100% = 100 × 0.01 = 1. You can always multiply a quantity by 1 without changing its value.

For throughput, just use the reciprocal of the n formula. For example, if you improve throughput from 1 thing/sec to 10 things/sec, then you've increased throughput by *new*/*old* = 10 times. As with n values, don't express this value as a percentage.

Note that a p value can never be bigger than 1 (or 100%) without invoking reverse time travel.[2] So, when someone tells you that their thing "improves response time by 1,000%," then you know they're not telling you a p value. It's probably an n value, meaning that their thing really makes your response time [merely] 10 times better than it was.

> *To say what sounds better, even though it's misleading...is not your best pathway to credibility.*

Here's my advice on the matter: whether you use the p formula or the n formula to describe your performance improvements, say also the *old* and *new* values, along with the name of the task you improved:

- "We improved T from 10 sec/exec to 0.1 sec/exec (99% reduction)."
- "We improved T from 10 sec/exec to 0.1 sec/exec (100× faster)."
- "We improved T from 0.1 exec/sec to 10 exec/sec (100× more)."

Communicating this way will ensure that your audience can understand what you've actually accomplished.

---

2 For a p value to be bigger than 1, *new* would have to be a negative number, meaning that your executions are so fast, they're finishing before they started.

90

The "n Times Faster" Myth

I cringe every time I hear it. A vendor says that if you'll upgrade to whatever it is that he's selling, then all your programs will run n times faster.

They won't.

You can hear it at the water cooler: "I heard we're going to upgrade to disks that are ten times faster than the ones we have today. Can you imagine our TPS report running ten times faster?!" "I heard we're going to upgrade to 1.5 times faster CPUs. Can you imagine PYUGEN running 1.5 times faster?!"

Oh boy. It's just not going to happen that way. Here's why. It's two reasons.

First, almost no program spends 100% of its duration using one and only one resource. Such a program would have a one-line profile, and you just won't see many of those. A program's profile will almost always have at least two lines in it, and probably way more. But I need only two to prove my point. So, imagine a profile that looks like this—let's call it the profile for program P1:

Resource	Duration
A	60
other	40
Total (2)	100

Then if you make resource A 2× faster, what happens to P1's profile? This:

Resource	Duration
A	30 ~~60~~
other	40
Total (2)	70 ~~100~~

P1 will run about 1.4× faster.[1]

Making resource A 2× faster is not going to make the whole program 2× faster; it's only going to make the resource A line in the profile 2× faster (from 60 to 30). The impact of the upgrade is going to be diluted by the fact that P1 uses more resources than just the one that was upgraded.

Now, for the second reason, let's look at some other program P2, whose profile looks like this:

Resource	Duration
A	10
other	90
Total (2)	100

How is the 2× faster resource A upgrade going to affect P2? Well, the users of P2 are going to feel cheated:

Resource	Duration
A	5 ~~10~~
other	90
Total (2)	95 ~~100~~

P2 is going to be only about 1.05× faster—nowhere close to 2×.[2] It's not because the upgrade was faulty; it's simply a mathematical inevitability. It's Amdahl's law. The upgrade to resource A helped P2 only in proportion to how much P2 used A to begin with, and P2 didn't use A much at all.

So there are two reasons that an *n*-times-faster upgrade is *not* going to make all your programs *n* times faster:

---

1 100 / 70 ≈ 1.4.

2 100 / 95 ≈ 1.05.

Dilution

A program's performance will improve in response to an upgraded resource only in proportion to how much that program uses that resource to begin with. The only programs that will be n times faster in response to an n-times-faster resource upgrade are programs that spend 100% of their time using the upgraded resource. You probably don't have many programs like that.

Different profiles

Different programs with different execution profiles will react differently to the same upgrade. So, there will be no single value of m for which you can say that after upgrading to an n-times-faster resource, everything is m times faster. Different programs will be different numbers of times faster.

It's skew, in both reasons.

Remember, I told you it's everywhere. Well, here it is again.

PART XII

Testing

91

Why Test?

Once, I visited a US government official who had just experienced a big project failure. He had just tried to roll out a new application that had been in development for five years. The rollout would begin in a classroom, where he had invited about twenty senior application users to see and use the new software for the first time ever. After the course, these advanced users would be responsible for disseminating what they had learned to the remainder of his department's roughly one thousand total application users.

But just a few minutes after the big unveiling, the sickening truth became clear: this system was so slow that it was unusable. It was supposed to serve a thousand users, but it couldn't even handle its first twenty.

How can an application miss that badly? Inadequate testing. It's two problems: one political and one technical.

The technical problem is that performance testing skills are rare. Certainly, if a feature's performance is bad enough, a developer might be able to see the problem in that feature's unit tests. For example, if a developer's new feature takes ten minutes to execute, even on a system with miniature test data and no load, then there's obviously a problem. But there are lots of performance problems you can't detect without both (1) realistic data volumes and (2) realistic traffic intensities. Knowing how to simulate a production environment requires skills that many application developers don't have.

The political problem is how difficult it is to reserve enough time at the end of a project to do adequate testing. That's because it's not just testing that you need to budget for: it's also the time it takes to fix whatever requirements, design, and code mistakes your tests end up implicating. The later you wait to test, the more time it takes. And that's not all. Even if a project's planners allocate enough late-phase time for testing and redoing, any schedule and cost overruns accumulated in earlier project phases tend to squeeze later project phases into smaller time and budget windows.

The solution:

- Create additional tests that measure how long features take to execute on a system with realistic data volumes and traffic intensities.
- Make these tests accessible to your developers *while* they're writing their code, so they can know right away when they're creating a problem.

Why test? So you can know how fast each feature in your application will run on your big, busy system. You test to learn where your system is weak, in time to do something about it.

Planning is not a substitute for testing.

Testing is also an opportunity to practice running the real system. System managers should test their software with the same tracing and profiling tools they'll use in production. Testing is a chance to become intimate with the performance of a business's high-priority tasks.

92

Risk

"Risk" is not just a qualitative label for plans that could go wrong. It is also a formal, mathematically defined term that helps project managers and investors calculate the expected value of a decision. *Risk* is the product of two factors: *probability* and *cost*. Probability, of course, is the likelihood that an event will happen, and cost is the pain you'll suffer if it does. You can think of risk generally in terms of four quadrants:

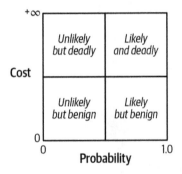

The top-left corner is where the most interesting conversations occur.

- Yes, the O-rings *could* lose their effectiveness in cold weather and jeopardize the vehicle, the crew, and the program. But the chances are slim, right?

- Yes, a fan disk in the #2 engine *could* disintegrate and sever the hydraulic lines in the top of the fuselage, which would cause loss of control of the aircraft. But what are the chances of that happening?

- Yes, our $5 million application *could* fail to support even twenty users in a classroom. But that would never happen, right?

93

Destructive Testing

Let's say that you think your system will have to support 1,000 users, so you create a test—a test, of course, with data volumes and traffic intensities that are as realistic as you can make them. And let's say you run that test, and the system performs just fine—all user experience durations are acceptable. OK, that's good. Of course. The fact that you have this kind of a test at all is a very good thing.

But what if the test data you've generated accidentally makes the conditions of your test easier than the conditions your application will face later in reality? What if the concurrent workload you've generated accidentally fails to reveal all of the coherency delays and queueing delays your application will face later in reality? There are lots of ways that a test can underrepresent the harshness your application will face in the real world. This, of course, increases your risk.

You can mitigate some of that risk by *testing to destruction*. For example, if you think your system will need to support 1,000 users, then don't just run your user count up to 1,000. Keep increasing the user count until your system breaks. Does your system break down with 1,017 users? Or does it not break until 7,132 users? These are two significantly different risk profiles, and you need to know which one is yours.

The same logic applies to your data. It doesn't matter whether you think your big table will top out at 25 TB, crank up the table size until your application breaks— or until you've tested such outrageous sizes that you're confident the app *won't* break because of your table size. Crank up your workload past your requirement to measure your headroom. It is valuable to know how much headroom your system has, and your tests can tell you. You just have to push them all the way to their failure points.

You should also use models that predict where your system will break.[1] You get a lot of predictive power when you combine good models and good tests.

Boeing tests to destruction when they design aircraft. They use big hydraulic jacks to bend their wings until they break. To certify an airliner for operation in the United States, the Federal Aviation Administration (FAA) requires for wings to be tested to 150% of the most extreme forces that an aircraft is expected to encounter during normal operations.[2] However, in some tests, Boeing will flex their wings all the way until they break. This tells them how much headroom they have beyond the 150% requirement, and it provides the data that engineers need to validate their mathematical models that predict what happens when wings break.

Testing to destruction makes decision making easier. And more reliable.

1 Gunther, "The Universal Scalability Law (USL)."

2 Jason Paur, "Boeing 787 Passes Incredible Wing Flex Test," *Wired*, March 29, 2010, *https://oreil.ly/ 08Dzv*.

94

Testing Is Not a Phase

It's a bad idea to relegate all of your testing to a separate phase at the end of a project. Testing needs to be an adversarial process, where the testers work as hard as they can to find defects and create reproducible test cases. Testing like this needs to happen continuously throughout a project, from the very beginning. Running your new system once at the end of your project just to show that everything works—well, that's not a test. That's a *demo*.

The biggest problems with testing at the end have to do with *time*:

- First, it takes a lot more time to fix a program you wrote ten months ago than it takes to fix a program you wrote yesterday. It takes time to get your mind back in context, and it can take even more time to deal with new interdependencies that have emerged in those ten months.

- Second, the final phase of a project is subject to the time-squeeze caused by all the overruns accumulated throughout that project's life. I've seen projects where "the squeeze" eliminated time for the testing phase altogether.

Bad things happen when you don't have adequate time to respond to unwelcome test (or demo) results. One of the worst is covert pressure from executives to stop finding so many problems. Such pressure can temporarily reduce your reported defect rate, but it serves only to pass more defects along to your end users, which hurts them and diminishes your reputation.

Fixing defects late in a project is a lot more expensive than fixing them early. A famous study documented by Barry Boehm showed that the cost of fixing software errors climbs exponentially the longer you wait.[1]

---

1 Barry W. Boehm, *Software Engineering Economics* (Englewood Cliffs, NJ: Prentice-Hall PTR, 1981), 40.

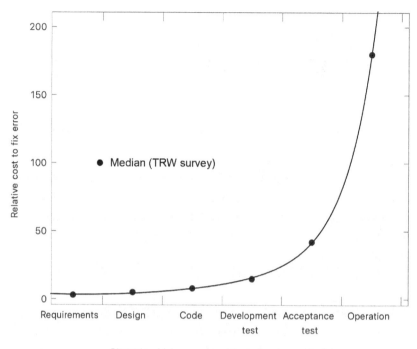

Phase in which error was detected and corrected

When you don't test until the end of a project, you can't find errors early in the project. Quality and cost both suffer.

95

Automated Testing

Automated software testing is a significant advance of the twenty-first century. I don't know how people do without it, honestly. Without automated testing, the world looks like this:

- A test is a big event. A big group congregates to "test the application." Each user runs the application as specified in a huge text document and makes notes about whether the application correctly performed each tested function or not.

- Developers and their managers are leery—if not outright scared to death—of making changes to the code, out of fear of collateral damage that may not be detected until the next big test, if ever.

With automated testing, the world looks a lot different:

- A test is hardly an event at all. You initiate a test simply by typing a command like `build test`. Every developer will run at least a portion of the overall test suite several times a day.

- Developers and their managers make code changes all the time, because they are confident that any unintended side effects will be detected immediately in the form of test failures. Developers then have the information they need to repair the collateral damage or, perhaps, negotiate a change in the specification to be memorialized into the test suite.

It takes a lot of work to create an automated test suite. It begins with a testing infrastructure that is imagined and built at the beginning of the project. The test cases themselves are built continuously from the software's initial requirements analysis, all the way through the end of the project. With thousands of automated tests, the tests may well account for as many lines of code as the actual application itself.

If you think of testing this way, it is unfathomable to think of doing this all at the end of a project.

Automated testing sounds expensive, but in practice I've found it's the other way around. With automated testing, I see companies get more done, at higher quality levels, with smaller teams, and less cost. It's a high-performance way to run a software development project.

96

Preventing Problems

Firefighting is sexier than fire prevention. Here's how you can tell: when's the last time you saw a TV series or a full-length feature film about the good people who install commercial sprinkler systems?

I didn't think so.

Hey, I fall into the same trap. Just look at the stories I've chosen to tell in this book. I have to compete for your interest, so I've selected the most interesting adventures I can remember.

But the even bigger truth is, I haven't just chosen these stories for my book, I've chosen these situations for my career. Finding and fixing other people's problems has made my life interesting, so I've sought those opportunities. Of course, many of the people I've helped would probably argue that they'd have been better off if their stories about performance had been a little *less* interesting.

The ability to fight yourself out of a problem situation has a lot of value. But it's also valuable to be able to prevent problems from happening in the first place. Wouldn't it be great to have both of those abilities? As it happens, the two abilities are pretty much the same, just executed at different times in the software life cycle.

You can prevent problems by doing the *look at it* thing earlier in your project. If you build a test system with realistic data volumes and traffic intensities, then you can use the same *look at it* method (Method R) that you would use to troubleshoot in production:

1. List the symptoms for which the business needs relief.

2. Sort the list into business-priority order.

3. For each symptom S in the sorted list:

4.   While further relief for S is your top priority:

5.   Observe S (*look at it!*), ideally, in the act of misbehaving.

6.   Find the cause C of the misbehavior.

7.   Relieve S by curing C.

Just like with production troubleshooting, you'll need to integrate some understanding about the business into steps 1 and 2. And, just like with production troubleshooting, that business integration may feel inconvenient at first, but it will help you keep your testing priorities aligned with the business's priorities.

Over time, the people who use the test system will begin to feel some of the same natural pressures they'd feel on a production system.

That report ran so long today; what did you guys change?

Ideally, you'll simulate enough pressure with your test systems early in your software life cycle that, by the time you go live, there won't be any surprises left.

PART XIII

Planning

97

Mrs. Utley

Mrs. Utley was my third-grade teacher when I was about nine years old. She taught us capacity planning. Here's one of the problems we worked on:

Imagine that you have $1. Write three ways you could buy items from the list below, leaving at least 25¢ in change. Write down how much change you have left.

Item	Price
Soda pop	15¢
Candy bar	10¢
Bubble gum	1¢

My answers would have looked something like this one:

Item	Qty	Price	Total
Soda pop	2	15¢	30¢
Candy bar	4	10¢	40¢
Total			70¢
Change			30¢

It was a clever problem to help train us for transactions that would happen nearly every day for the rest of our lives. To do the problem:

- We had to grok the overall concept of trading one resource for another.
- We had to convert between $ (the unit for the stuff we had) and ¢ (the unit for the stuff we wanted).

- We had to add and subtract—and multiply, if we wanted to finish earlier.
- We had to formulate a way to communicate our answer back to the teacher so she could use the information. (Her particular use was to evaluate how well we had learned to do the problem.)

These are exactly the things you have to know, to do capacity planning.

98

Capacity Planning

Capacity planning is complicated and hard, especially for CPU planning. It's difficult to predict how much resource an application that you've never run in real-life before is going to consume. Fortunately, we live in the age of the *elastic cloud*, in which vendors like Amazon and Oracle can sell you the amount of CPU you need to get going, and then they can adjust your CPU capacity to your needs without having to physically move your application from one computer to another.

Even with this tremendous technology at your disposal, it is still important to be able to see a program you care about in a systemwide context. Here is a model that helps you do that.

	A	B	C	D	E
1	CPU Capacity Model v1.1 (2020-10-26)				
2					
3					
4	Capacity Model for Monday 2:00p peak hour				
5					
6	business function	run/hr	CPUsec/run	CPUsec/hr	% capacity
7	WENUS Report	1	3,600.000	3,600	25%
8	TPS Report	4	200.000	800	6%
9	Book Order	1,200	0.800	960	7%
10	Other	1		0	0%
11	Total			5,360	37%
12					
13	Capacity (4 cores)			14,400	100%
14	Spare capacity			9,040	63%

In this model, the shaded cells are where you'd type your input, and the white cells are all computed. It's just Mrs. Utley's problem, but with different nouns.

Item	Qty	Price	Total
WENUS Report	1	3,600	3,600
TPS Report	4	200	800
Book Order	1,200	0.8	960
Other	1	?	?
Total			5,360
Change			9,040

- Instead of having the capacity of a dollar, this system has a capacity of 4 CPU × 60 sec/min × 60 min/hr = 14,000 CPUsec/hr (cell D13).

- The run/hr column (B) contains the quantity data. These values are how often the business wants to run each business function during the Monday 2:00 p.m. peak hour.

- The CPUsec/run column (C) contains the price data. You learn these prices by tracing.

- The CPUsec/hr column (D) is the total CPU consumed by each business function. CPUsec/hr = run/hr × CPUsec/run.

- The change left over (D14) is the total CPU capacity (D13) minus the capacity consumed by your business functions (D11).

- Column E is just the total capacity consumed expressed as a percentage. It's like pretending you have a dollar's worth of CPU (E13), and then perceiving the WENUS Report as costing 25¢ (E7).

- Row 10 is a recognition that you probably don't want to model every single program that runs on the system during the Monday 2:00 p.m. hour. I certainly wouldn't advise it. But if you know your actual CPU utilization for that hour, you can use the Microsoft Excel *Tools › Goal Seek...* feature to make cell E11 match your observed utilization, by changing cell C10.

- Cells F11 and F14 give you helpful advice, in an effort to try to keep you away from the far right of the hockey stick curve that shows you how bad queueing delay can get if you overdo your traffic intensity.

A model like this is important for completing the mental image of a system as a list of things that are running, all presumably helping your business, and all exerting a cost upon the capacity you're paying for every day. Imagining your system in this form can help you decide which programs are the most important to try to optimize.

Once again, you'll help everyone on the system if you can negotiate the quantities in column B downward or if you can reduce the costs in column C.

Optimizing always comes back to our two dear friends:

1. Reduce the event count, or

2. Reduce the mean duration per event.

99

Utilization Targets

I like to tell the (fictional) story of the man who retired and moved to upstate New York. He and his wife—let's call them Brad and Vonda—had always imagined running a little B&B up on Otsego Lake near Cooperstown, where the Baseball Hall of Fame is. With the nest egg they had saved, they bought a little place and realized their dream. It went better than they had ever imagined. They had ten guest cabins that were routinely booked to capacity. They were having the time of their lives and making more money than they had made from their "real" jobs. They appreciated the irony of that.

One evening, Brad and Vonda were enjoying a warm drink with some of their guests when there came a knock at the door. A man in a suit explained that the famous entertainer, Jennifer something (pick your own favorite), was outside in the car. She had heard so many nice things about the B&V B&B that she wanted to spend the night, along with a three-person entourage. What a fun opportunity! Of course, they'd love for Jennifer to stay the night. Maybe she'd talk about the reunion or sing a song or something. There's just one catch: the B&V B&B is *full* tonight. There's no room!

On a computer, sometimes you may have periods where your workload is completely predictable. In such a case, we say that your request arrival process is *deterministic*. Some systems have deterministic arrival periods at night, for example, when the online users have all gone home and a batch scheduler keeps the CPUs running at a perfect, surge-free 100%.

However, on a system with a *random* arrival process, the arrivals tend to clump together, which makes managing your capacity more difficult. There will be periods when no requests arrive at the system, and then there will be periods when dozens of requests all arrive, inconveniently, all at the same time. The lulls waste resource capacity, but the spikes waste users' time.

At the B&V B&B, when a room goes empty for a night, the revenue opportunity for that night is lost forever. Mainframe batch managers used to say, "When a cycle goes idle, it's gone forever." But when your arrival process is random (nondeterministic) and you still want to accommodate everybody, then you have to leave some headroom. The question becomes *how much?* Because headroom has a price.

You probably won't get the whole answer from a mathematical model, but it's important to remember that queueing has a hyperbolic effect upon response times. You'll want to choose a utilization target that's low enough to make your system sufficiently responsive but high enough that you don't waste too much of the capacity you've paid for.[1]

---

1 Or, equivalently, a traffic intensity target.

100

When to Upgrade

Here are some thoughts to consider about hardware upgrades:

Benefits

There are lots of good reasons to upgrade your hardware. You get faster equipment, better vendor support, and more options for running newer software releases. Hardware upgrades *feel* good. And eliminating calls may not sound all that good if you've tried and failed, or if you've paid somebody a lot of money to try and fail.

Limits

A radical technology upgrade (from disk to SSD, for example) might make a 10× or a 100× difference in a component's response time. But a hardware upgrade will never solve a ramp problem, and faster hardware isn't going to help you wait any faster for that lock being held by your colleague who's running a faulty sales report. The highest leverage improvements, say, 1,000× or more—I've even seen a 1,000,000,000× improvement—are going to come from event count reductions.

You can't hardware yourself out of a problem that you've softwared yourself into.

Costs

Upgrading hardware obviously carries a direct cost, but additionally, there's potential for increased software license fees, and there's the project cost of moving your applications and data to the new system and testing everything to make sure you're happy with it. The cost of changing a job schedule or an algorithm is often significantly less.

Risks

The Payroll story illustrates one reason you should *test* your hardware upgrades. It's especially important to test, if your hardware upgrade implies software changes, too.[1]

Other options

Most people expect hardware upgrades to make everything on the system a little bit faster. But what many people don't realize is that if you're operating with high traffic intensities, then eliminating unnecessary events from even just one program can make everything else on the system a little faster, too. With profiles, you can predict such effects.

Absence of other options

Sometimes, you can't reduce your event counts. Maybe the skills to do it aren't accessible. Maybe your application vendor won't cooperate. Or maybe there just aren't any more wasted events in there to eliminate. When you've eliminated all the unnecessary events you can, and your application is still too slow, then upgrading your hardware is your next option.

You may be able to improve performance by upgrading your hardware, and in some cases that will be your best option. But look, too, for opportunities to reduce your event counts. You might be able to make a bigger impact more quickly and less expensively. Plus, if you keep your application software lean and trim, then when you do get to upgrade to better, faster hardware, you'll be more apt to fully enjoy the experience.

---

1 Remember, the upgrade in the Payroll story was bug-free, and it *still* caused a problem.

PART XIV

Politics

101

Proving

There's a joke about a guy who was looking for his car keys outside in the dark one night. A friend who was walking by joined in to help him. After looking together for several minutes, the friend, trying to be helpful, asked the guy where he thought he probably was when he lost them.

"Oh, I dropped them somewhere over there."

"Then," the friend said automatically, "why are we looking over *here*?"

The guy pointed up at the light and said, "Because there's no light over there."

...People are like that.

I use a spicier version of that story, in hopes you'll remember it better:

> *When your keys are in the sewer, you're never going to find them in the flower pot.*

When your prescription for solving a problem is hard—meaning expensive, time-consuming, politically risky, or just inconvenient—you're going to have to provide compelling proof of *two* things:

1. The hard thing you're prescribing is actually going to work; and

2. There's nothing easier that would also work.

Without compelling proof (and sometimes, sadly, even *with* compelling proof), people will do the easy thing every time. But if an awful-sounding solution is the only *actual* solution, then trying anything else is a waste of time. If your keys really are in the sewer, then the sooner you put your gloves on and start digging, the sooner this whole thing will be over with.

Proof is important to your reputation as well. Realize: if you've convinced people to dig around in a sewer, then those keys had better damn well be there. So proving helps the people around you make well-informed decisions, *and* it also helps you protect your credibility as an advisor.

102

The Problem with Underpromising

I think every consultant I've ever met has tried to abide by the mantra that you should always "underpromise and overdeliver." It must be something they teach in Consulting 101 courses all over the world. The idea is that if you underpromise and overdeliver, you'll end up exceeding expectations and looking like a hero. That's the theory anyway. There's a problem, though, which I can illustrate with a story.

Andy and Barney both optimize programs for a living. They're competing against each other for a lucrative project, so they each propose an estimate of the value they expect to create. Andy estimates that he'll be able to make an important program go two times faster. He believes he'll do better than that, but caution and humility restrain his estimate. What Andy doesn't know is that if he were to win the project, he would make the program go *seven* times faster.

Barney estimates that he'll be able to make the program go *three* times faster, and on the basis of this estimate (because three is better than two), he wins the job. Barney is not as good at optimizing as Andy is, but he makes the program go three times faster—just as he'd promised—so the client is happy. The client doesn't know, of course, but they would have been better off—and certainly Andy, the better optimizer, would have been better off, too—if Andy had been a better estimator.

103

Seven Project Risk Magnifiers

If you're a consultant, one of the choices you have to make (or that someone has to make for you) is whether to accept a given project. Certainly there are some projects you're better off saying no to. I can't tell you which ones those are, because the go/no-go decision is a function of the skills available to you and your individual tolerance for risk. The way to decide whether to take on a project is to assess its risks and then measure your aversion to those risks. I can help by listing some of the risks I have learned to look out for:

Prospect's goal: artifacts or relief?

During your discovery process, you need to learn the prospect's overall aim: are they engaging you just to check a box on a checklist? Or are they engaging you to make actual improvements to their situation? If the prospect's aim is just to have you create a report and not actually change anything, that's fine, but you need to know this up front. Straining against the bridle of wanting to make a difference but not being allowed to: that increases risk in your project.

A focus on project artifacts like reports and documentation tends to increase your project duration and risk. A focus on working together to create results tends to decrease your risk.

Prospect's bias: prejudicial or receptive?

It's normal for prospects to have preconceptions about the causes of their symptoms. But if all their preconceptions were correct, then they probably wouldn't need you. The degree to which your prospect is committed to their preconceptions is important. Are the theories and methods they had in mind before they met you the only theories and methods they're willing to believe? If they're not going to let you trace, for example—for me—that's a showstopper. Skepticism is healthy, but distrust isn't good for a project.

Steadfast, unwavering commitment to a preconception, even in the face of evidence to the contrary, tends to increase your project duration and risk. Willingness to evaluate and accept new ideas tends to decrease your risk.

Prospect's culture: political or technical?

One of our goals for creating Method R was to eliminate guesswork—to give business leaders the best possible information for their decisions about system performance. The method works best in an environment where curiosity, truth, and solutions (a just culture) are valued more highly than fear, policy, and blame (a blame culture).

Maybe you'll hear sentiments like, "I can tell you in advance, if your 'findings' recommend doing x, it is *not going to happen*." So then, what will you do if your analysis proves that (1) doing x will reduce this company's highest priority's duration from an hour to a second, and (2) there's no way other than doing x to get even close to that amount of benefit?

More bureaucracy, more policy, more stakeholders, difficulty in determining a single point of responsibility for a system…these all increase your project risk. More decentralization, more freedom, and more willing accountability all decrease your risk.

Prospect's mood: panic or calm?

When you solve problems for a living, you're going to meet people with problems. However, the magnitude of a team's panic (which is almost always inherited from its leader) may or may not be proportional to the magnitude of the crisis at hand. Some leaders can remain calm in the face of the worst imaginable crisis; others seem to believe that their teams are incapable of productive action unless they've first been set on fire.

More panic, more worry, more time pressure…these all increase your project risk. More calm, more stability, and more faith all decrease your risk.

Prospect's attention level: neglectful or attentive?

During your work, you're going to need resources from your client. Among the most important is simply *attention*. The right kind of attention helps you get things you need, like time from DBAs and developers who can help you test your ideas. You don't want your hard work to go into a filing cabinet; you want it to go into improving the system.

Neglect increases your risk. Healthy attentiveness decreases your risk. Of course, not all attention is good attention. Unwanted attention—driven by suspicion, politics, or panic—increases risk.

Prospect's self-awareness: illusory or self-aware?

Low-ability people often lack the self-awareness to recognize their own ineptitude. The particular cognitive bias wherein people of low ability suffer from illusory superiority is called the *Dunning–Kruger effect.*

Dealing with illusory superiority is tricky. For one thing, it can be difficult to tell who is suffering more from the effect. Is it the prospect? Or is it *you*? After all, your prospect might know a lot more about his own system than you do, so I encourage you to challenge yourself about it.

The path forward is the data. But sometimes getting the right data can take more time and effort to gather than an impatient client with illusory self-superiority is willing to wait for. People in the unskilled–unaware quadrant increase your risk.

Access to authority: inaccessible or accessible?

A prospect's authority model can range from centralized to distributed. It's tempting to believe that more centralization means more risk for you, because more centralization generally creates decision-making bottlenecks that will delay your work. But the important factor is not so much the amount of centralization of authority as it is your *access* to authority. With centralized authority, your risk is actually low if you have a good relationship with the central authority. Distribution of authority can make it easier for you to make progress, too, if you have *access*. It is *access* that is key.

Lack of access to authority will increase your risk. Trustful relationships with people who can facilitate your progress decrease your risk.

104

Fail Fast

Among movements like Agile, Lean Startup, and Design Thinking these days, you hear the term *fail fast*. The principle of failing fast is vital to efficiency, but I've seen project managers and business partners be offended or even agitated by the term *fail fast*. I've seen it come out like, "Why the hell would I want to fail *fast*?! I don't want to fail at *all*." The implication, of course: failing is for losers—if you're planning to fail, then I don't want you on my team.

I think I can help explain why the principle of *fail fast* is so important, and maybe I can help *you* explain it, too.

Software developers know about *fail fast* already, whether they realize it or not. In 2006, I blogged about an example.[1] It had been a really long day. I didn't leave my office until after 9 p.m., and then I turned my laptop back on as soon as I got home to work another three hours. I had been fighting a bug all day. It was a program that ran about 90 seconds normally, but when I tried a code path that should have been much faster, I could let it run fifty times that long and it *still* wouldn't finish.

At home, I ran it again and left it running while I watched TV, assuming the program would finish eventually, so I could see its log file (which I wasn't flushing often enough, which was another problem). My MacBook Pro's fan was running so loud that my son asked me if it was OK. The whole time, I was thinking, "I wish this thing would fail faster." And there it is.

When you know your code is destined to fail, you want it to fail faster. Debugging is hard enough as it is, without your stupid code forcing you to wait an hour just to see your log file, for the evidence you need to go fix something. If I could fail faster,

---

1 Cary Millsap, "Fail Fast," blog post, May 13, 2006, *https://oreil.ly/Zhl4N*.

287

I could fix my problem sooner, get more work done, and ship my improvements earlier.

But how does that relate to wanting my *business idea* to fail faster? Well, imagine that a given business idea is in fact destined to fail. When would you rather find out?

a. In a week, *before* you invest millions of dollars and thousands of hours into the idea?

b. Or in a year, *after* you've invested millions of dollars and thousands of hours?

I'll take option *a* a million times out of a million. It's like asking if I'd like a crystal ball. Um, *yes*.

The operative principle here is "destined to fail." When I'm fixing a reported bug, I know that once I create a reproducible test case for that bug, my software will fail. It is *destined to fail* on that test case. So, of course, I want my process of creating the reproducible test case, my software build process, and my program execution itself to all happen as fast as possible. Even better, I wish I had come up with the reproducible test case a year or two ago, so I wouldn't be under so much pressure now. Because seeing the failure earlier—failing faster—would have helped me improve my product earlier.

But back to that business idea. Why would you want a business idea to fail fast? Why would you want it to fail at all? Well, of course, you don't *want* it to fail, but it doesn't matter what you want. What if it is *destined* to fail? It's really important for you to know that.

So how can you know?

Here's a little trick I can teach you. Your business idea *is* destined to fail. It is. No matter how awesome your idea is, if you implement your current vision of some nontrivial business idea that will take you, say, at least a month to implement, not refining or evolving your original idea at all, your idea will fail. It will. Seriously. If your brain won't permit you to conceive of this as a possibility, then your brain is actually increasing the probability that your idea will fail.

You need to figure out *what will make your idea fail*. If you can't find it, then find smart people who can. Then, don't fear it. Don't try to pretend that it's not there. Don't work for a year on the easy parts of your idea, delaying the inevitable hard stuff, hoping and praying that the hard stuff will work its way out. Attack that hard stuff first. That takes courage, but you need to do it.

Find your worst, most likely showstopper, and work on that first. If you cannot solve your idea's worst problem, then get a new idea. You'll do yourself a favor by killing a bad idea before it kills you. If you solve your worst problem, then find the next one. Iterate. Shorter iterations are better. You're done when you've proven that your idea actually works. In reality. And then, because life keeps moving, you have to keep iterating.

That's what *fail fast* means. It's about shortening your feedback loop. It's about learning the most you can about the most important things you need to know, as soon as possible.

So, when I wish you *fail fast*, I mean it as a blessing, not a curse.

105

Face

"I just made the TPS report 10,0000 times faster!" You're ecstatic, and for good reason. You can't wait to tell somebody. You run to your client's department director's office, and you tell her exactly what you did: "I just made the TPS report 10,0000 times faster!"

"That's great," she tells you. But she doesn't seem as happy as you thought she'd be. And then she asks who wrote that code. Still jubilant, you tell her. Your enthusiasm now begins to evaporate as it dawns on you what's going on. Next thing you know, she's on the phone with that developer's manager, telling him she wants him in her @#$%&! office. *Now.*

You didn't realize you were starting an avalanche, but you're in it up to your ears now, because you didn't think just *one* move ahead. Now all you can think is how much you wish you could rewind ten minutes and play this hand a little differently.

Here's an alternate story. Your first meeting wasn't the department director; it was the developer who wrote the TPS report program. You show him how you found the 10,000× improvement opportunity. He gets it. You learn that he and his colleagues had also made the same mistake in three other reports, so, wow, the success story is going to be four times better than you originally thought.

You go to the department manager's office together. The message is that you *and the developer* have found a way to make four reports, including TPS, 10,000 times faster. You've already scheduled a brown-bag lunch meeting for Thursday, where you and your colleague will share your technique with the broader development team. The future is bright. You're still a hero, and now you have a new ally on the development team.

My friend Anjo Kolk taught that performance problems are 90% political and 10% technical. Anjo's worldview was influenced by having worked on a long project in

Japan, where the concept of *face* is magnified by Japanese culture. It is important in *every* culture to consider the honor and reputation of the people who work around you. You have to realize that every time you fix something, you create the implication that someone else screwed up. In some cultures, the pain this causes can be unbearable.

In the US, where I've done most of my project work, the prevailing business culture is mostly to honor facts over feelings, but there's a spectrum of attitudes about dealing with failure. Some company cultures embrace failure as an inevitable step along any sufficiently audacious path. Others prioritize avoiding blame at any cost.

The Netherlands (where Anjo is from) is fondly prominent in my mind as a culture of just saying the truth, no matter how painful the words might feel. Of course, the road goes both ways. I find Dutch candor refreshing, but I also have to remind myself not to be sensitive if a Dutchman tells me to take off my "fokking sweater" when nobody's hot but me. And I have to remember that the Dutch feel impatient when I wrap my point in too many words.

Candor requires responsibility. Effective candor is not just blurting out every unvarnished thought that comes to your mind; it's saying the truth only after you've carefully determined what the truth really is. So, don't proclaim that everyone around you is an idiot, when the real truth (and more useful discovery) might be that all these people are doing exactly what they've been trained to do.[1]

There are lots of resources available that can help you develop your skills for succeeding in the face of cultural and political impediments. Here are two that I especially recommend:

- The Wikipedia article on *crew resource management* (CRM),[2] the airline industry's highly effective response to a string of fatal accidents in the 1970s whose causes were found to be not technical problems but problems with interpersonal communication, leadership, and decision making—the kinds of things I mean by *political problems.*

- Liz Wiseman's book, *Multipliers: How the Best Leaders Make Everyone Smarter* (Harper Business, 2017). "Just imagine what you could accomplish if you

---

1 That happens a lot in my Oracle work, where hardly anybody is ever trained to do the *look at it* thing that I think is so important.

2 "Crew resource management," Wikipedia, *https://oreil.ly/JZfa5*.

could harness all the energy and intelligence around you." Liz's book will help you get there.

Really optimizing requires attention to both technical and nontechnical elements. Getting ahead of yourself on one or the other can be detrimental to you and those around you.

106

The Jeweler's Method

I learned about the *Jeweler's Method* from one of my early mentors within Oracle, my dear friend Dave Ensor. It goes like this…

A man tells his wife that he will accompany her today to the jewelry store, to pick out something nice for a special anniversary. He has saved $200, and this is how he intends to use it. Hugs and kisses all around—this is going to be fun! At the store, a nice jeweler greets the couple and, after listening to their story, leads them to the case with the $200 rings and bracelets and necklaces.

As the husband and wife are discussing the pieces they like the most, the jeweler says, "I'm sorry to interrupt, but these just came in yesterday, and they're just so exciting that I want you to see them," motioning to a counter farther to their right. The wife obliges, making her way down to this other counter, as the husband continues to peruse the $200 items.

Moments later, he looks up and notices his wife admiring herself in a mirror, wearing a bracelet from the new collection. The jeweler remarks, truthfully, "Isn't it lovely on her wrist?" The husband agrees, but he can't help noticing the price tag. The bracelet from the new collection costs, oh no, $300. But he sees how happy it makes her, and he realizes that now, not buying that bracelet amounts to taking it away from her.

Here's how the Jeweler's Method can work for you…

The program that Phyllis runs every day is too slow. After studying the problem, you learn that creating a new database index and dropping another will fix Phyllis's problem. You test carefully, and you determine that the likelihood of collateral damage to other programs on the system is small. However, you know that the DBA team is unlikely to implement your recommendation because of some bad experiences they've had before.

So you invite Phyllis over to your workstation. You offer her a chair and ask her to please run her slow program on the test system where you've been experimenting. She runs her program, and it finishes in a split second. She turns to you. "It didn't work," she says. "This program takes more than three minutes to run. It can't be giving the right answer."

You ask her to check, to make absolutely certain.

As she runs the program a couple more times and studies the output, you can hear the crescendo of joy in her voice as she discovers, "No, this is exactly right, this program is running just fine, and it's taking less than a second to run! This is wonderful!"

So, you ask, "Can you please run this other thing, too, just to make sure that I didn't accidentally do anything to slow it down?"

She runs the other program. "No, this is just as fast as it ever was. Maybe faster. I'm so excited! Thank you...*so* much!"

"Well, but there's a problem," you tell her. "I can fix your slow program in the test system, as you've seen. But your company's change control procedures prohibit me from making the same change on your production system. I'm going to need your help convincing your system managers to make this change."

She nods. She doesn't want the joy she's just experienced to be taken away. "I know exactly who I need to go talk to," she says. "I'll be back in touch soon." You notice that instead of walking back to her desk, she's walking toward the CFO's office. You have a new teammate who's going to help you get this done.

107

Change Control

To improve a company's system, you'll have to navigate that company's *change control* policies. Change control is like an immune system designed to protect a system from harmful changes. But change control is an impediment if it unreasonably delays you from making helpful changes, especially when a system is in trouble.

It's fine for change control policies to delay changes on a happy system. But when a system is in crisis, you may have to sacrifice safety for agility. For example, my client in Orange County would have died by Friday if their change control policies had delayed our ability to eliminate that table lock or fix a bunch of bad SQL. But their CEO cleared the way for us, realizing that policies and procedures exist to support the business, not the other way around.

Change control can be particularly frustrating for short engagements. You may recall, I got only a week at most of the clients I've visited. If a change control policy slowed me down by even a day or two, then I might be gone before anyone could implement my suggestions. Sometimes clients would tell me half a year later at a conference, "No, we never got around to replacing that index. Yeah, the TPS reports are still really slow..."

That's sickening news when you're trying to make a difference. This is why techniques like the Jeweler's Method are so important. Inspiring an advocate in the business who will keep up the pressure to fix things is better than just writing a recommendation.

108

Record Keeping

In 2016, Jeff and I worked on a project near Richmond, Virginia, where users were running on a system that was slower than it needed to be because they hadn't written something down. They had done several experiments over the course of many weeks that resulted in kind of a foggy recollection of what worked and what didn't:

- "I think I remember it being really slow when we set parameter P1=false."
- "I think I remember it being fast when we set parameter P2=3."

By organizing the experiments they had done into a structure called a *factorial experiment matrix*, we could derive more value from their work:

	Parameter value		Response time
	P1	P2	(seconds)
1.	true	1	284.7
2.	true	2	78.4
3.	true	3	4.2
4.	false	1	
5.	false	2	9.9
6.	false	3	154.7

Since P1 had two values that they had wanted to test and P2 had three, the matrix calls for six different experiments. As you can see, they had done only five.

The structured data was harmonious with what people thought they remembered:

- "...Slow when P1=false" is confirmed in experiment 6.
- "...Fast when P2=3" is confirmed in experiment 3.

But the ultimate verdict that they had chosen, of P1=false and P2=3 resulted in the response time for their program being 154.7 seconds instead of the 4.2 seconds that was possible. And, of course, without doing another test, none of us could know whether the program would have finished even more quickly using the parameter values called for in experiment 4.

I know that it feels like writing slows you down, but it doesn't. Nothing does more than writing to improve the quality of both your actual work and the communications about your work:

- Sometimes you remember things wrong. It happens. Written records are more accurate than remembered ones.

- Organizing and indexing your research structures your thinking, which helps make sure that you're spending your time answering the right questions...*all* the right questions (like alerting you to the fact that nobody had ever executed experiment 4).

- Cross-referencing your evidence helps you make your arguments more airtight (consider using the *Bates numbering system* that attorneys use).

- Written records can be shared, studied, and learned from.

- Your writing defines how your work will be remembered. I teach my staff:

If it's not written down, then it didn't happen....
At least not the way you'll remember it.

Literally, of course, I mean that if you don't write it down, then you're going to have a much more difficult time *proving*—to both others and yourself—that it happened.

One of the hazards of disorganization is wasting time working on the wrong thing. In Richmond, one of the problems we solved was discovering that one of their main concerns—where they had spent loads of time worrying—wasn't actually a problem at all. They had thought that some queries were slower after an upgrade, but they actually weren't. They had the evidence, but they hadn't organized it.

Proving what was really happening freed them to work on other high-priority symptoms that were real problems to be solved. It sounds completely crazy, but it happens more often than you might think. It speaks to how complex our jobs can get sometimes.

109

Failure

I've worked hard in this book to give you lots of tidy little stories to learn from, each with its own tidy little happy ending. Do you know why all the endings are happy? It may not be what you think…

It's because I get to choose which stories I tell.

Not every story in my career has had a happy ending. There have been a few unhappy ones, but not too many. Most of the ones that I ended up feeling bad about were situations where I was certain that my team knew the right thing to do, but we just couldn't convince our client to do it. Getting people to do the right thing is almost always the hardest part of a project.

When you think about the short stories in a book like this, please remember that these events I've written about didn't happen instantaneously, or without loads of setbacks along the way. For example, Richard's story—such a clean little snap-tight story—took you probably less than 15 minutes to read, but the job we did in that story took four people working full-time (and a few others part-time) *three and a half days to do.*

I can remember sitting with Richard after almost three hours of grinding, trying to find and isolate the trace data we needed, and wondering how much longer he was going to let us keep trying. Fortunately for everyone's sake, he wanted relief and he was receptive, technical, calm, attentive, self-aware, and accessible: he scored a perfect 7 on my "Project Risk Magnifiers" checklist. He could have put up his hand at 10:30 the first morning and said, "Enough's enough, I don't have time for this," and the project would have ended in failure. Instead, he asked good questions and brought us ice cream while we worked.

Your success level usually includes some factors over which you have no control. In retrospect, I can see that all my success stories have had four things in common:

1. They had setbacks where failure felt imminent.
2. They had some factors that were beyond my control.
3. I had help.
4. I didn't quit.

Recognizing these points helps me formulate the following prescription:

1. Don't be afraid. Trust your preparation. If you don't trust your preparation, then invest into better preparation.
2. Remember the serenity prayer. You need the *serenity* to accept the things you cannot change, the *courage* to change the things you can, and the *wisdom* to know the difference.
3. Find people who can help you. Develop relationships with them. It's an important part of your preparation. Don't be shy about asking for help.
4. Don't quit.

110

Don't Worry,
Be Nervous

On April 12, 1981, test pilot and rookie astronaut Robert Crippen lay on his back in the pilot's seat of Space Shuttle Columbia, awaiting the liftoff of mission STS-1, the new vehicle's first test flight into space.

Although Crippen had never flown to space before, his preparation for this mission had been immense. He had a degree in aerospace engineering. He'd been a naval aviator for 20 years, a test pilot for 17, an astronaut for 15, and a member of the shuttle design team for more than 10.

Also on his back, in the seat left of Crippen, was mission commander John Young, who by this time had flown in space four times and even driven a car on the moon. Crippen told the story of how his much more experienced commander had helped him cope with the bit of nervousness he was feeling in the moments before liftoff.

"I knew it had its potential dangers, but a lot of things in life do," Crippen said. "As John told me, he told me: 'OK Crip, any time they're getting ready to light off seven-and-a-half million pounds of thrust under you and you aren't a little bit anxious, you don't understand what's going on.'"[1]

I love this story. It demonstrates that it's natural to feel nervous, even when you're prepared. Even when you're an astronaut. Don't fear being nervous. Try to embrace it as your body's gift of extra strength and focus for dealing with a meaningful event.

---

1 "STS-1: 'A Test Pilot's Dream,'" CNN.com, April 14, 2006, *https://oreil.ly/fMmDj*.

PART XV

Just for Fun

111

Optimizing for Kids

This Richard Feynman quote is important to me:

If you can't explain it in simple terms,
then you don't understand it.

I also like to share problem-solving stories with my family. It's good practice, and sometimes they find the stories interesting. Especially when it's companies whose names they recognize, like Amazon or Apple or 7-Eleven. When my kids were little, I played a game with them to help them understand what their Dad does for a living. You might enjoy playing this game with your family, too.

The game begins with the premise that when Mom goes to the grocery store, it takes only about half an hour. But one day, Mom wasn't home and Dad had to go buy the groceries. And it took him almost *four* hours! Eight times longer than Mom. Wasted half a day. *This*—no doubt—is a performance problem. A serious one.

I ask them to pretend that they're performance consultants who'll get paid piles of cash if they can help fix this problem for me. So I ask them how they'd begin helping me. Here's what happens: they start shouting out ideas for how to make my trip to the grocery store faster. Before they have *any* idea how I do it. This is hilarious, because it's exactly what the grownups do! They can't even make it through listening to me say what the symptom is before they start shouting out recommendations for how to relieve it.

So I coach them a little bit. And it's *hard*. I try to get them to think about the big picture of "What process are we going to use to help this guy?" but they've already defaulted to the process—without actually *deciding* anything—that we're just going to shout out ideas that might help.

They're down, rolling around in the *possible causes* space, while I'm trying to help them understand that they need more clarity about the *symptoms* before they can really help me. I'm dying for one of them to say some kind of *look-at-it*–oriented comment like, "Well, take us with you, so we can *see* how you do it," or "Can you describe to me what you did when it took you four hours?" But they just won't say it.

I realize that this, also, is just like the grownups. The *look at it* idea doesn't seem hard to me now that I know how great it works, but to be fair, I logged a lot of high-stress hours before I figured it out, so maybe it's just simply not obvious. I hope that you're different now that you've read this book. That would be nice.

So, back to the kids, I can't get them where I want them to be until I just come out and tell them, hey, why don't you offer to come along with me on my shopping trip, and then you can tell me what's wrong, *based on what you see*. Except instead of actually going to the grocery store, let's just pretend the whole trip, here in the living room. Instead of really going, I'll just tell you all the steps I took, and you can ask me any questions you want.

OK. We can do it that way.

Excellent. So I've gotten them to agree to tracing my trip.

"OK," I say, "here's what I do. I look at the list on the microwave [the little magnetic notepad we keep there], and it says 'bacon.' So I walk to the grocery store to buy bacon."

"Whoa-whoa-whoa," I can hear all the kids say in unison: "Mom doesn't walk. She takes the car. That's your problem."

Just like the grownups: (1) it's always the hardware, and (2) silver bullet.

"OK," I say, "so I take *the car* to the grocery store. Yes, I can see how that would save some time. The grocery store is about a 15-minute walk from the house, but it's only a couple minutes by car. Got it, thanks, so that'll save a lot of time." (Notice that you can't know how much time it will save, because you don't have a *profile* yet—just a little bit of the trace data. You'll see.)

I say, "Alright, so here's how it goes. I look at the list that says 'bacon.' I drive to the store and park. I go in. I find the bacon. Then I pay for the bacon, come back to the car, and drive home. Then I look at my list, and it says 'eggs.' I drive to the store..."

"Whoa-whoa-whoa," they say. "No, you don't get one thing at a time. You take the list *with* you to the grocery store!"

"What?!" I say.

"No, you make just one trip. You get everything in one trip."

"Oh!" I say, "That's going to *really* speed things along. OK, so I drive to the grocery store, *with the list*." Nods. "I park, look at the list, 'bacon,' go in, buy bacon, pay for it, take it to the car, look at the list, 'eggs,' go back in..."

"No!" everybody screamed. "You don't get just one thing at a time, you get *all* the things and then pay out only once."

"How am I supposed to carry all that stuff?"

"With a shopping cart!"

"A *what*?" (This game is more fun with *little* kids.)

"A shopping cart! Those wire basket things with the wheels on them? Those are for you to push around with all your stuff in them. So you get all your stuff on your list, and then you push your cart up to one of the self-checkout things— never mind Dad, *you* should probably go to one of the people that ring it up and bag it *for* you. You'd never know what code to type in for your peppers."

With their help, we arrive pretty quickly at a much-improved process for buying groceries. We even get into how it'll probably still take me a little bit longer because I don't know where all the items are in the store as well as Mom does. If we really wanted to optimize that, we'd make me a map of the store. Those are the kinds of things we ended up discussing, which was fun.

Then they asked me what this had to do with my job. Do I help people shop for groceries for a living?

"No, I *explain* things for a living," I told them. "My job is to figure out where the opportunities are to make things go faster, and then I explain how people can take advantage of those opportunities. One common pattern I see is processing just these little tiny fragments of stuff on each 'round trip' between you and some computer a thousand miles away, instead of processing bigger loads for each trip."

So then we get to talk about how a network is kind of like the road in my story, and how servers are kind of like grocery stores, and how an inefficient algorithm on a server is kind of like not using a map in the store, and so on.

Try it sometime. Teach some kids to *look at it*.

I hope you'll have as much fun with it as I have.

Glossary

algorithm

A finite sequence of well-defined, computer-implementable instructions, typically to solve a class of specific problems or to perform a computation.

Amdahl's law

A mathematical model used to find the maximum expected improvement to an overall system when only part of the system is improved.

antipattern

A commonly occurring attempted solution to a problem that generates decidedly negative consequences.

Bates numbering

A referencing system used in legal, medical, and business fields in which each individual line in an arbitrarily large set of documents is uniquely identified for rapid retrieval.

bottleneck

The resource that dominates the response time for a given task execution.

capacity

The amount of a resource that is available to provide service in response to requests for service.

cause

A reason for a condition or action.

cell

A single data element within a table, which belongs to exactly one column and one row.

change control

The policies and procedures that govern how changes can be applied to a system.

client

1. A person or company to whom a vendor is providing a service. 2. Hardware or software that accesses a remote service on another computer.

coherency delay
> The duration that a request spends waiting for data to become consistent (coherent) by virtue of point-to-point exchange.

column
> A vertical group of cells within a table.

central processing unit (CPU)
> The electronic circuitry that executes the instructions comprising a computer program.

crew resource management (CRM)
> The effective use of all available resources for flight crew personnel to assure a safe and efficient operation, reducing error, avoiding stress, and increasing efficiency.

critical path
> The sequence of tasks determining the minimum time needed for an operation.

cure
> To relieve a symptom by addressing its cause.

customer
> A person or company to whom a vendor is providing a product.

database
> A collection of tables.

database administrator (DBA)
> A specialized computer systems administrator who is responsible for managing and maintaining one or more databases.

deterministic
> Predicable with certainty.

DTrace
> A performance analysis and troubleshooting tool that is included by default with various operating systems, including Windows, Linux, and macOS.

enterprise resource planning (ERP)
> A type of software that organizations use to manage day-to-day business activities such as accounting, procurement, project management, risk management and compliance, and supply chain operations.

experience
> The collection of observable results of a single execution of a task.

first-come, first-served (FCFS)
> A queue discipline that provides the next unit of service to the earliest request in the queue, regardless of its class of service. Also called *first-in, first-out (FIFO)*.

glossary
> A textbook appendix in which an author works largely beyond the scrutiny of his editor to define terms in whatever manner he believes might marginally improve reader satisfaction.

Goodhart's law

The observation that when a measure becomes a target, it ceases to be a good measure.

hard disk drive (HDD)

A secondary storage device that uses rapidly rotating platters coated with magnetic material, paired with magnetic heads, usually arranged on a moving actuator arm, which read and write data to the platter surfaces.

histogram

A two-dimensional data structure in which the independent dimension consists of nonoverlapping intervals, and the dependent dimension represents the count of elements within each interval.

instrumentation

Instructions that are inserted into a program's control flow in order to measure that program's performance.

interprocess communication (IPC)

A mechanism an operating system provides to allow processes to manage shared data.

load

Competition for a resource induced by concurrent task executions.

local area network (LAN)

A computer network that interconnects computers within a limited area such as a residence or office building.

loss aversion

The tendency to prefer avoiding losses over acquiring equivalent gains.

Mathematica

An integrated software system with built-in functions covering all areas of technical computing.

mean

The average of a list of numbers, computed as the sum of the values divided by the count of the values.

measurement intrusion effect

A type of systematic error that occurs because the execution duration of a measured program is different from the execution duration of the program when it is not being measured.

Method R

A reliable, deterministic, finite method for optimizing a system.

M/M/c

A mathematical model used to predict response times, queue length, and other features of a system having c homogeneous, parallel, independent service channels, where arrivals are determined by a Poisson process, job service times have an exponential distribution, there is no restriction of queue length, and the queueing discipline is first-come, first-served.

Moore's law

The observation that the number of transistors in a dense integrated circuit doubles about every two years.

OpenTelemetry

A collection of tools, APIs, and SDKs that you can use to instrument, generate, collect, and export telemetry data (metrics, logs, and traces) for analysis in order to understand your software's performance and behavior.

optimize

To maximize the economic value of some target.

percentile specification

A specification of performance expectations of the form, "Task t will respond in less than or equal to r units of time in at least proportion p of executions."

performance

The time it takes to execute a task, measurable directly as either response time or throughput.

preemptive multitasking

A scheduling algorithm that uses a centralized scheduler to preempt a running task execution so that an awaiting task execution can have its turn consuming resources for a predetermined time interval.

priority

A ranking of importance.

profile

A tabular decomposition of response time, typically listed in descending order of component response time contribution.

program

A sequence of computer instructions that carries out some business function.

prospect

A person or company with whom you might like to do business, but who is not yet a client or a customer.

queueing delay

The duration that a request spends enqueued at a given resource, awaiting its opportunity to consume that resource.

ramp

A performance antipattern in which experiences gradually worsen over time.

random

A property of a sequence of values that are not deterministic but follow an evolution described by a probability distribution.

ratio fallacy

A deficiency inherent in any ratio that permits the performance of a system being measured to become worse while the apparent goodness of the ratio value improves.

resource

A service provider, such as a device or a subroutine call, whose participation in an execution's response time can be measured.

response time

The duration of an experience.

risk

Uncertainty about future benefits or costs, quantified using probability distributions; the product of probability and severity.

row

A horizontal group of cells within a table.

scalability

The rate of change of response time or throughput with respect to some specified parameter.

scheduler

An operating system subroutine that is responsible for allocating CPU cycles among competing processes.

scheduler interrupt

An event caused by an interval timer that instructs the CPU to run the operating system scheduler subroutine.

sequence diagram

A type of graph specified in the Unified Modeling Language (UML), used to show the interactions between objects in the sequential order that those interactions occur.

service channel

A resource that shares a single queue with other similar resources.

skew

Nonuniformity in a list of values.

solid state drive (SSD)

A secondary storage device that uses integrated circuit assemblies to store data persistently. They are quieter, more shock resistant, and faster than physical spinning disk drives.

span

In the OpenTelemetry standard, a span is a named, timed operation that represents a piece of the workflow in a distributed system. Multiple spans are pieced together to create a trace.

strace

A Linux utility that shows a record of system calls executed by programs on Linux systems, used for diagnostic, instructional, and debugging purposes.

surrogate measure

A measure that isn't what you need but is easy to obtain and seems related to what you need.

symptom

A feature regarded as indicating a problem, particularly such a feature that is apparent to the business.

table

A collection of data, arranged into horizontal rows and vertical columns, with the column values generally representing attributes of each row.

task

A business unit of work, such as a click, a report, or a batch job.

throughput

The count of task executions that complete within a specified time interval.

Tow–Millsap law

An observation that no user wants to see more than about ten rows in a query result.

trace

A stream of output that lists the steps that a process is executing.

traffic intensity (ρ)

Utilization divided by the number of service channels, resulting in a measure of load confined to the range $0 \leq \rho \leq 1$.

tune

To manipulate a system in an attempt to improve its performance.

universal scalability law (USL)

A mathematical model used to predict throughput without requiring detailed internal system measurements the way that typical queueing models do. USL is an extension of Amdahl's law.

utilization

Resource usage divided by resource capacity for a specified time interval, resulting in a measure confined to the range $0 \leq u \leq c$, where c is the number of service channels.

vendor

The provider of a product or service to a customer or client.

waste

Anything that can be eliminated with no loss of utility.

wide area network (WAN)

A telecommunications network that extends over a large geographic area.

Yeti

In the folklore of Nepal, an ape-like creature taller than an average human that is said to inhabit the Himalayan and Siberian regions of East Asia. The scientific community has generally regarded the Yeti as a legend, given the lack of evidence of its existence.

References

Boehm, Barry. *Software Engineering Economics*. Englewood Cliffs, NJ: Prentice Hall PTR, 1981.

CNN. "STS-1: A Test Pilot's Dream." April 14, 2006. *https://oreil.ly/fMmDj*.

Erlang, Agner K. "Sandsynlighedsregning og Telefonsamtaler" [Probability Calculation and Telephone Conversations], *Nyt Tidsskrift for Matematik* (in Danish), 20 (B): 33–39, JSTOR 24528622, 1909.

Fleming, Matt. "A Thorough Introduction to eBPF." LWN.net, December 2, 2017. *https://lwn.net/Articles/740157*, 2017.

Goldratt, Eliyahu, and Jeff Cox. *The Goal: A Process of Ongoing Improvement*. Great Barrington, MA: North River Press, 1992.

Gunther, Neil. "How to Quantify Scalability: The Universal Scalability Law (USL)." *https://oreil.ly/EKKfY*, 2020.

Gunther, Neil. *Guerrilla Capacity Planning: A Tactical Approach to Planning for Highly Scalable Applications and Services*. Berlin: Springer, 2007.

Gunther, Neil. *The Practical Performance Analyst: Performance-by-Design Techniques for Distributed Systems*. New York: McGraw-Hill, 1998.

Jain, Raj. *The Art of Computer Systems Performance Analysis: Techniques for Experimental Design, Measurement, Simulation, and Modeling*. New York: John Wiley & Sons, 1991.

Kleinrock, Leonard. *Queueing Systems Volume 1: Theory*. New York: Wiley-Interscience, 1975.

Millsap, Cary. *The Method R Guide to Mastering Oracle Trace Data*. Southlake, TX: Method R, 2019.

Millsap, Cary. "Fail Fast." *Cary Millsap* (blog), May 13, 2006. *https://oreil.ly/GR8lL*.

Millsap, Cary. "The Ramp." *Cary Millsap* (blog), April 29, 2010. *https://oreil.ly/-mPmh*.

Millsap, Cary. "What Happened to 'When the Application Is Fast Enough to Meet Users' Requirements?'" *Cary Millsap* (blog), February 27, 2015. *https://oreil.ly/-sFOY*.

Millsap, Cary, and Jeff Holt. *Optimizing Oracle Performance: A Practitioner's Guide to Optimizing Response Time*. Sebastopol, CA: O'Reilly, 2003.

ProjectManager.com. "The Ultimate Guide to the Critical Path Method." *https://oreil.ly/7vCin*, 2021.

Rosen, Christine. "The Myth of Multitasking." *The New Atlantis*, Spring 2008. *https://oreil.ly/junNL*.

Shortle, John, James Thompson, Donald Gross, and Carl Harris. *Fundamentals of Queueing Theory*. New York: Wiley, 2018.

Wikipedia. "Amdahl's law." *https://oreil.ly/8egXt*.

Wikipedia. "Crew resource management." *https://oreil.ly/kHttD*.

Wikipedia. "Spherical cow." *https://oreil.ly/NsmXw*.

Wiseman, Liz. *Multipliers: How the Best Leaders Make Everyone Smarter*. New York: Harper Business, 2017.

Index

About the Author

Cary Millsap spent the 1990s learning a lifetime's worth of technical and political lessons as a traveling consultant for Oracle Corporation. He and the teams of performance specialists he recruited and trained at Oracle helped hundreds of customers around the world. In 1999, he co-founded a company called Hotsos, which became renowned for its annual performance-focused symposium event. In 2008, he founded Method R Corporation, which has served many of your favorite brands and created the world's first software system for managing, mining, and manipulating thousands of Oracle trace files. Cary and colleague Jeff Holt were named *Oracle* Magazine's 2004 Authors of the Year for writing *Optimizing Oracle Performance*. He is the author of *The Method R Guide to Mastering Oracle Trace Data* and coauthor of *Tracing Oracle*. He has helped to educate thousands of information technology professionals through his commitment to writing and teaching. He is published in professional journals including *Communications of the ACM*.

Colophon

The cover illustration is original art created by Susan Thompson. The cover fonts are Guardian Sans Condensed-Medium and Gilroy Semibold. The text font is Adobe Minion Pro; the heading font is Benton Sans; and the code font is Dalton Maag's Ubuntu Mono.